THE
MARTIAL
ARTS

THE
MARTIAL
ARTS

By Susan Ribner
and Dr. Richard Chin

Drawings by Melanie Arwin

HARPER & ROW, PUBLISHERS

New York, Hagerstown, San Francisco, London

The Martial Arts

Text copyright © 1978 by Susan Ribner and Richard M. Chin
Drawings copyright © 1978 by Melanie Gaines Arwin

First Edition

Library of Congress Cataloging in Publication Data
Ribner, Susan.
    The martial arts.

    SUMMARY: Presents the history, philosophy, and meaning of the most well-
known and popular martial arts.
    1. Hand-to-hand fighting, Oriental—Juvenile literature. [1. Hand-to-hand
fighting, Oriental] I. Chin, Richard, date, joint author. II. Arwin, Melanie Gaines.
III. Title.
GV1112.R53 1978   796.8'15   76–58713
ISBN 0–06–024999–4
ISBN 0–06–025000–3 lib. bdg.

CONTENTS

THE
MARTIAL
ARTS

INTRODUCTION

Centuries ago in China a small old man with a long beard was walking through the woods, leaning on a gnarled walking stick. At a turn in the path he found three bandits attacking a poor peasant who was on his way home from market. The old man approached the bandits slowly and said in a soft but firm voice, "Stop. Leave that man alone."

"Go away, old man. Mind your own business!" commanded the leader of the bandits, a towering, bearlike man.

Calmly the old man replied, "Don't you know that if you do evil, evil will come back to you?"

"Stop preaching, old man, or I'll smash you like this," said the huge man, and kicked at a nearby tree, smashing it in half.

The old man smiled faintly. "I do not fear you," he said.

With that, this headstrong bandit lost his temper and kicked out at the small man. Seemingly without effort, the old man brushed aside the kick, and the bandit went crashing on his back in the dust.

The second bandit, a tall, wiry woman with piercing eyes, drew her sword and rushed toward the old man. She slashed at the man's head, but before she completed the move, the old man had already moved out of range. The woman turned around to see the third bandit, who had tried to tackle the old man's legs, go flying through the air and land in a big puddle of mud.

The three bandits, now outraged at this humiliation, growled, cursed, made fierce faces, and attacked the old man all at once. But the little man could not be touched, and the three bandits landed in a heap, one on top of the other.

Realizing that they were in the presence of a master, the three fell to their knees and begged the old man to forgive them. "Take us as your students, please, teach us what you know. Teach us how to fight."

"I cannot teach you my fighting art," said the old man, "for this art cannot be given to those who will use it to bully other people. The martial arts are for those of good character who will protect people from bullies like you. In fact, if you do not have the right attitude, I could teach you for the rest of my life and yours, and you still would not comprehend this art."

But the three bandits continued to plead, and promised they would change their ways and give up their bandit lives. After they apologized to the much-relieved peasant, the bandits and the old man walked off into the woods together.

We do not know what became of the three bandits, but we do know that what happened in this story is symbolically important in the history of the martial arts. For this old man was a kung fu master of the Shaolin monastery. Around the year A.D. 600, he and other monks and nuns of that order—some of the greatest *kung fu* masters of their time—developed the fighting arts in ways never attempted before, and in a

Monks practicing Horse Stance.

manner that profoundly influenced the martial arts as we know them today.

According to legend, about 1500 years ago, in A.D. 525, a Buddhist monk traveled several thousand miles from India into China, walking alone over the Himalayan Mountains, through forests filled with wild animals, through swamps, over unbridged rivers. His name was Bodhidarma, and he was to found what is now known as Zen Buddhism.

After receiving permission from the Chinese emperor to remain in China, Bodhidarma traveled to a Buddhist monastery in Honan Province. This monastery, hidden away in the middle of a green forest, was called *Shaolin*, meaning "young forest." Here Bodhidarma began to instruct the monks in his way of Buddhism, but he found that they were so weak from their inactive life in

4

the monastery that they would fall asleep during the meditations he was trying to teach them. So Bodhidarma proceeded to give the monks certain exercises to make them healthier and stronger, telling them they could never become spiritually strong if they were physically weak.

These new exercises—special hand movements, body positions, and breathing exercises—also turned out to be useful as self-defense techniques. One of the exercises the monks practiced, for example, was standing in a special position called Horse-Riding Stance (Horse Stance, for short). It was called this because the position resembles how one looks sitting on a horse—both legs wide apart, knees bent, and back straight. The Shaolin monks practiced this exercise by standing in Horse Stance for as long as one hour at a time.

5

Through this training the monks developed good balance and exceedingly strong legs. They discovered that when they were attacked by bandits who traveled the countryside preying on "helpless" monks, they were not so helpless anymore. Their balance was so good and their legs so strong and rooted to the ground that bandits couldn't easily push them around. This is why the old monk in the story could not be knocked down.

Along with the physical training, the monks did mental exercises. The Horse Stance, for example, was also done as a "meditation" exercise. This meant that while the monks were holding this position, they had to concentrate very hard on one particular thought. They could not let their minds wander even though this exercise was extremely boring. They also could not move, no matter what. If they had an itch, they could not scratch it. If a mosquito landed on their forehead, they could not swat it. The pain was even worse, for holding a sitting position without anything to sit on is very painful indeed. The monks had to learn to conquer this pain, to make their minds so strong they could endure it.

With this disciplined training the monks developed such good concentration and such keen awareness of their surroundings that sometimes they had a "sixth sense" about things. If they were attacked by bandits, for example, they could almost see what the bandits were going to do before they moved. In addition, people who had endured months of pain and struggle with the Horse Stance would be unlikely to crumble under the pressure of actual fighting situations. It was training such as Bodhidarma's mental exercises that gave the old man in the story such sharp awareness of his enemies' movements, as well as his exceeding calm in the face of such danger.

And so, through the practice of Horse Stance and many other similar exercises, the fighting arts gradually became an important part of the Shaolin monks' everyday training, and the monks became strong and fearless fighters who could easily handle any bandit foolish enough to attack them.

As the years passed the monks devised new and better fighting techniques. They refined the ancient hand-to-hand fighting methods which had, before this time, often required brute strength to be successful. The new approaches, developed by trial and error, used faster and more efficient movements aimed at achieving the best results with the smallest amount of effort. This is called using "technique," and explains why the little old man in the story could easily defeat fighters who were younger, stronger, and larger than he was. This is why today, since most martial arts rely upon use of good "technique," they can be practiced successfully by all people regardless of size, age, or sex.

But it is not for superior fighting alone that we remember Shaolin, for many women and men throughout Chinese history have made important contributions to fighting technique. There was something more.

Up to this time in China people had studied fighting methods only to enable themselves to defeat their enemies. They learned fighting in order to fight. This was changed by the arrival of Bodhidarma and the close connection that developed between fighting and Buddhist practices.

It should be remembered that the Shaolin fighters we are discussing were first and foremost Buddhist nuns and monks. They spent their days in meditation and study of the Chinese classics, seeking perfection of character. The ultimate aim of their strivings was to reach a certain spiritual state of mind called *enlightenment*. While it is quite impossible to explain in words, enlightenment might be akin to experiencing feelings of oneness with the universe, a marvelous sense that everything with you and the world is just as it should be.

The practice of fighting exercises, then, was an integral part of this quest for enlightenment, and as such it was clearly a means toward higher ends rather than just an end in itself. It is because of this concept that Chinese fighting practice evolved into an art form, marking the beginning of the martial arts as we know them today.

When the monks and nuns did find it necessary to defend themselves, a moral code now accompanied their fighting practice. As Buddhists, they followed certain ideas of loyalty, respect, and honesty toward each other, and strove for attitudes of unselfishness and benevolence toward the world at large. It was considered wrong to fight indiscriminately. One was not supposed to use fighting skills, for example, to get more money or better clothes, or to show off one's technique. Instead, fighting was to be used for self-defense purposes or to help others. This code explains why our legendary old monk had the humanity to refrain from doing unnecessary harm to the bandits of the story.

Fortunately for us, these new concepts did not remain hidden in the green forests of Honan. The training methods spread to other Shaolin orders of nuns and monks. The fame of these practitioners also spread, and people came from all over China hoping to be accepted for special training in the martial arts. Monks and nuns traveled throughout their country, which was then riddled with civil war and banditry. They taught the people Shaolin fighting styles so they could defend themselves against injustice, and they spread their Zen Buddhist teachings in the hopes of bringing peace to China. In this way Shaolin kung fu spread throughout China, to be refined and expanded by other masters in later years.

In time the Shaolin nuns and monks also traveled throughout Asia—to Okinawa, Korea, and Japan, spreading their philosophy and with it their martial-arts knowledge. Each people adapted the teachings to its own culture and needs, and developed from its new knowledge many different martial arts. What all the arts retained, however (even the modern martial arts such as *judo*, *karate*, and *aikido*), was the underlying philosophy of Shaolin—that the martial arts are a means for developing physically, mentally, and spiritually, and not just a fighting method for defeating one's enemies. It is this philosophy that has made the difference between ordinary street fighting and the true martial arts.

1 KUNG FU

Kung fu is a Chinese expression which means "work, something which takes much time and effort to accomplish."

We don't know how or why it happened, but in recent years Westerners began to call the Chinese martial arts kung fu. Perhaps this was because learning any martial art takes a long time and much hard work. The Chinese terms for these arts, however, are *wu su*, the classical term for military or self-defense arts, and *gwo su*, a more recent phrase meaning national or Chinese arts. In this book we will use the popular term, kung fu. It does not refer, as many believe, to just one style or art, but rather to all the many Chinese martial arts.

HISTORY

The origins of kung fu are obscure and probably start at the dawn of Chinese history when the first person consciously picked up a stick or rock to defend against danger, either from animals or other humans. We do not know exactly when this was, for it was before there were books or writing. The earliest written records we do have are of people fighting against animals. Almost five thousand years ago the legendary king of China who was called the Yellow Emperor was supposed to have defeated a monster with his bare hands.

Over the next four thousand years, Chinese society

became increasingly complex, constantly torn by wars and other internal conflicts. People from feudal warlords to small farmers, from housewives to bandits, storekeepers to painters, and even children learned to fight for survival and, sometimes, for personal gain. Many were great warriors, and the Chinese of today remember fondly many of the heroic fighters of their early history.

One such warrior was Shuen Guan, who lived during the Jinn Dynasty (A.D. 265–384). This thirteen-year-old girl could fight so well with swords, spears, and her bare hands that she was nicknamed "Little Tigress." One day when her town was attacked by a group of bandits, she was the only person courageous enough to fight her way through the bandit group and go for help to a neighboring general, Sheh Lan. The general was so impressed with Shuen Guan's bravery that he agreed to help her. The girl, the general, and his troops returned to her town, where they fought together to drive out the bandits, who never dared to return. For her courage Shuen Guan was honored by her town, and by the emperor of China as well.

Such heros, of which there were many, have given kung fu its richness and variety. Yet as sophisticated as the methods of fighting used by warriors became over the years, it was not until Bodhidarma's arrival at Shaolin, some two hundred years after Shuen Guan, that the fighting arts gained a unique spiritual and artistic flavor that distinguished them from the fighting arts of earlier years. The Shaolin order became the hub of kung fu activity in China for more than a thousand years, and while many other fighting systems developed at the same time, Shaolin was by far the most famous.

For some time only those who were nuns and monks learned the Shaolin arts, but the fame of Shaolin and the constant civil turmoil in China ended this isolation. During the Ch'ing Dynasty (1644–1912)—a dynasty of foreign Manchus who had invaded China from the north, overthrown the Chinese Ming Dynasty, and taken control—many officials and supporters of the Ming fled into hiding to avoid persecution by the Ch'ing officials. They shaved their heads, donned monastic robes and, disguised as monks and nuns, hid out in Shaolin monasteries where they were welcomed by the anti-Manchu Shaolin people. Here they secretly plotted the overthrow of the Manchus and the restoration of the Ming.

The Manchus were fooled for a while, until a former Ming official informed them of these secret plans. Excellent fighters themselves, the Manchus gathered their forces, surrounded the Shaolin monastery at Honan, attacked, and finally burned it to the ground. Today movies are made and stories told and retold of how the few heroic martial artists who escaped spread out underground to all parts of the country. Some built new monasteries, others traveled from place to place, and most began teaching their arts to select villagers, hoping to unite the people in an uprising against the foreign conquerors.

Over the next century the Chinese people did revolt against the Manchus time and time again, often with martial artists in their ranks. Finally, in 1730, an edict, or law, was passed forbidding the practice of the Chinese martial arts. For a while it looked as though kung fu had completely disappeared, but in fact, the arts were being practiced secretly in homes, fields, and caves. Knowledge of the martial arts was passed down quietly from parents to their children and to their children's children.

Many years later martial artists emerged once again in a fight against foreign invaders. In 1900 kung fu practitioners who belonged to various secret societies, such as The Society of Righteous and Harmonious Fists, spearheaded a revolt against a new group of foreigners, this time the Western powers, who were attempting to control China and divide up her wealth for their own purposes. This famous event was called the Boxer Rebellion—*Boxer* is a name often used for the Chinese martial artist.

The Boxers, however, were badly defeated. Later, the Manchu empress of China turned on them, executed their leaders, cleared out the kung fu training halls, and drove the martial artists underground once more. Many fled China as a result.

This event served to strengthen the foreigners' hold over China, and to varying degrees, foreign countries, including the United States, controlled China thereafter until 1949, when the armies led by Mao Tse-tung and Chou En-lai finally put an end to foreign rule.

While China's chaotic history certainly caused kung fu knowledge to spread out from the confines of the Shaolin monasteries, the actual number of competent practitioners always remained quite small. Although the

Chinese soldiers as pictured in Illustrated Times, *1857.*

Shaolin masters were interested in teaching the martial arts for revolutionary purposes, they were nonetheless still very secretive about their skills, and very selective in their choice of students. They knew that the martial arts, a most beautiful thing in the hands of a master, could be very destructive in the wrong hands.

And if few Chinese were taught, even fewer foreigners had this privilege. With this history of secrecy, plus the years of abuse by Western powers, it is no wonder that up until the late 1950's no Westerners to speak of were taught the Chinese martial arts. It wasn't until the 1960's and 1970's, with the new Western interest in Eastern culture—art, philosophy, and medicine, for example—that change began. The West finally heard about kung fu and, to put it mildly, went wild. Kung fu movies, comics, magazines, TV programs, and pictures of Bruce Lee currently flood the country. Yet the tradition of secrecy that still prevails at many kung fu schools, even in this country, has meant that media information about the martial arts is often incorrect. The following pages will reveal some of the wonders of kung fu, and correct some of the misconceptions about these marvelous arts.

TRAINING

During the height of the Shaolin monastery's fame many people flocked to the doors of the temples hoping to learn the secrets of the famed fighting arts. The difficulty in obtaining entrance—the exceptional strictness with which the Shaolin took students—serves as an example of most traditional kung fu training.

Hopeful women and men, boys and girls, waited outside the monasteries for days on end. Only those who returned, day after day, waiting patiently through the hot sun or heavy rains, showing their true desire to learn, were admitted. When these dedicated few were finally taken into the monasteries, the real testing began.

For the first six months or so students could be found not on the exercise floor, but out in the forests, gathering plants and tree barks to be used for teas and medicines, farming in their rice paddies and gardens, slicing up *baktoi* and other vegetables for dinner, and scouring rice out of huge pots. They scrubbed floors and also studied Chinese classics and Buddhist scriptures. These daily chores were designed to educate the students, make them well rounded, and further test them for humility and patience—virtues essential to kung fu.

If students did not balk at washing thousands of dishes, did not sneak off to sleep in the lush woods instead of searching for herbs, and did not become over-anxious to begin their martial-arts studies, then they were finally accepted into the formal self-defense training.

When the students first arrived for practice, they were taught the special training etiquette—how to bow to their teachers (called *sifu*s in Chinese), how to address senior students, and how to conduct themselves in class. Then, most often, practice began with what is called *stance training*.

Stance means the special way one stands—the foot, leg and body position of a person. In kung fu, depending upon the particular fighting style being taught, there are from five to ten stances that are considered basic to a style. In much the same way, sports like football or baseball have special basic stances: One stands a certain way for blocking in football, and another way for batting in baseball. In classical ballet there are five basic foot positions, or stances, that all beginners learn. These basic positions in dance, football, baseball, or kung fu are always practiced and used, no matter how advanced or professional the practitioner is.

In Shaolin kung fu (as already mentioned) one basic posture was called Horse Stance because the practitioners looked as though they were sitting on horses. Another was called White Crane Stance since the student balanced on one leg like a crane. Cat Stance was still another, the person's legs imitating the hind legs of a cat about to spring.

While there were many such stances, training often began with Horse Stance and, following the tradition of Bodhidarma's days, the students would be expected to hold Horse Stance without moving until a stick of incense finished burning—often as long as one hour. Trainees would practice only this exercise for six months or a year without being taught any other techniques.

While these lessons may seem strange to us, they served many important functions. As explained earlier, Horse Stance training not only strengthened the students' legs, but also tested their endurance and patience, and at the same time began to build character and discipline. People who know many flashy fighting techniques but have no character, no patience, and no stamina will crumble in a crisis and their techniques will be worthless.

Stance practice, however, meant not only standing in one position for a long time, but eventually meant training in movement. Students began to learn how to move forward and backward, stepping into Horse Stance each time. They did this slowly at first and then faster until the movement became as effortless and natural as walking. Other stances were practiced in the same way, and in time students learned to change from one stance to another while moving—changing, for example, from Horse Stance to Crane and then back to Horse again until this, too, became second nature to them.

Stances, indeed, are the foundation of the martial

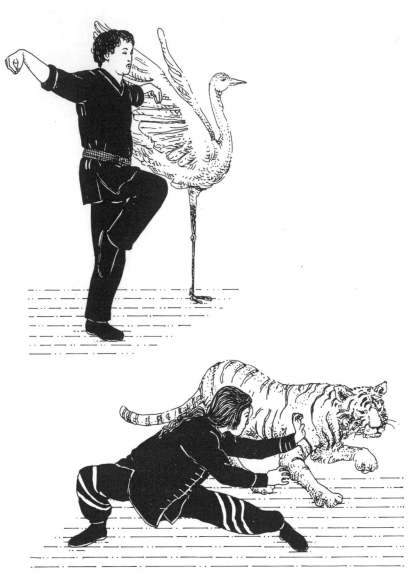

White Crane Stance (top); Cat Stance (bottom).

arts—similar to the roots of a tree. Yet as the roots of a tree are usually hidden from the observer, so too is the purpose behind stance training often not seen by new students. Finding training boring and painful, many often quit at this stage of training. Overanxious to know everything at once—to taste the fruits and see the flowers of a full-grown tree, as it were—they often fail to recognize that kung fu—like the tree—must begin slowly, down in the dirt, and only after this foundation has been set and a long period of growth has taken place will the tree bear fruit and blossom.

If the students did finish this difficult training, they were then introduced to other basic kung fu techniques. They learned to use their arms and hands—how to make a fist and do hand motions such as grabbing, punching, and blocking. Gradually they were taught to coordinate hand motions with stances—for example, to step into Horse Stance and punch at the same time.

Next, sifus would explain how to use feet and legs. Trainees learned what parts of the foot could best be used as weapons. They were taught to kick with the sides, the heel, and the ball of the foot rather than with the toes, which break easily. They learned different kinds of basic kicks, some to the front, some to the side, and others to the back.

When students reached a certain level of achievement in these basic movements, they were then taught *sets*. A set is a choreographed or prearranged series of movements that is memorized by the student and then practiced again and again with exactly the same sequence of moves each time. In this respect a set resembles dance or gymnastic floor exercises. A kung fu set, however, includes strikes, blocks, and kicks, along with various stances, and is designed to increase coordination, speed, and power.

Students were taught two types of sets: solo sets in which they performed alone against imaginary opponents, and dual sets with partners, in which one person performed as the attacker and the other as the defender, both working with prearranged movements. There were many sets to learn, and as students improved their skills they were taught increasingly complicated and difficult sets.

Students usually did supplementary exercises like running to increase their breathing power and leg strength. They did plenty of stretching to give themselves flexibility, making movement easier and lessening the chance of injury. Students often did weight training to increase their strength, lifting light weights many times in a row. Weight training should not be confused with weight lifting—lifting hundreds of pounds at one time; or with muscle building—lifting weights to develop muscles primarily for looks.

After two or three years of this difficult Shaolin training program, students often developed new misconceptions about kung fu. They were now in good condition, quite strong, and beginning to beat some of the other students in matches. Feeling invincible, sure they now knew most of what there was to know, some quit at this stage.

Others, however, wisely continued with advanced training, where they now encountered some of the older masters. As old and weak as they appeared physically, they were able to play with these youngsters as effortlessly as a cat plays with a mouse. Humbled by this experience, the students quickly realized there was certainly more for them to learn, and even more to learn after that. It was at this point, when they realized that there was really no end to training, that they finally began to learn kung fu. For kung fu is much more than just self-defense techniques. It is an art form, a way of life, a means toward spiritual development. As such, kung fu is a lifetime study.

While modern-day training usually does not involve waiting on streets for admission to schools, cooking meals for sifus, and doing Horse Stance for six months (although sometimes it does), the feeling and methods of training are essentially the same as they were centuries ago in Shaolin. All martial-arts training, in fact, involves heavy emphasis on stance training, constant repetition of basic movements, and years and years of hard work. It is for this reason that bullies do not ever get seriously into kung fu, for the lessons take too much time, and a bully would rather buy a weapon at a local store and go quickly about his work of bullying. If for some reason bullies kept up training for a long period of time, they would probably be transformed, for the effect of extensive kung fu training is to make the practitioner a better person.

Weapons Training

Today, as in the past, once students have developed a certain proficiency in the basic techniques of kung fu, they are usually introduced to weapons training. Weapons have always been an important and integral part of kung fu, and people still train in those same weapons used centuries ago in China, though the original purpose for their use may have long since passed.

The weapons practiced are as varied in shape and size as they are numerous. Many, such as the sword, bow and arrow, and spear are military in origin. Others—the scythe, sickle, and pitchfork—were farm tools used by peasants in ancient China who had to improvise when faced with sudden attacks from bandits and marauders. Similarly, fishing people fighting for survival on the sea

Various weapons, including spear, swords, three-piece rod.

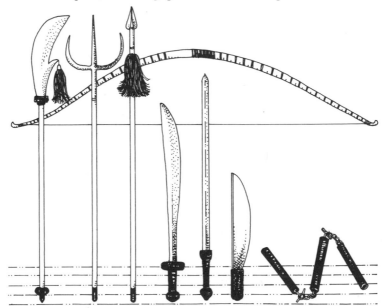

used oars and nets as weapons. Perhaps the most common weapon was the staff, or stick, used for carrying burdens or simply as a walking stick. A comparable weapon today might be an umbrella, cane, or a pocketbook.

Weapons training is essentially the same as training without weapons, only now weapons are used as an extension of the hands. Students practice basic strikes and blocks with their weapons in the same fashion that they practiced their bare-hand techniques. Good stances are, once again, essential. And in time, students progress to weapons sets. While training with scythes, swords, sticks, and oars is always difficult and repetitive, it is, nonetheless, always challenging and exciting.

Iron Palm and Ch'i Training

In addition to weapons training, advanced students are often taught special techniques such as *iron palm* and *ch'i* development. Many kung fu "feats" performed by masters of iron palm and ch'i have spread myths of the magical powers of the Chinese martial arts. Such feats, however, are performed not by magic or trickery, but by skills that have taken years of hard training to develop. They are no less marvelous because of this.

The origins of the iron palm technique, like those of many kung fu techniques, are obscure. We do not know who originally developed the technique, or when it was created, but we do know that it has been practiced in the Chinese martial arts for centuries. Training in iron palm is usually done in the following way: Students begin by repeatedly thrusting their hands into a bucket of very fine sand. They practice daily, and after each session treat their hands with special medicine to keep them soft. (It is a myth that martial artists need to deform their hands by developing huge knuckles and calluses.) When the students become used to the sand, they graduate, using the same techniques, to a bucket full of small pebbles, then small rocks, and finally iron filings or ball bearings. When they can finally strike full force into iron, then they have what is known as the iron palm or iron hand. This training can be dangerous, and should only be practiced under the direction of a qualified instructor. It cannot be accomplished without the use of special herbal medicine that will prevent serious injury to the hands.

One famous master of the iron palm was Pak Sing, head of the Pak Sing *choi li* system. Until his death in the 1960's Pak Sing demonstrated his iron palm skill throughout China and Taiwan. This small man, who weighed not more than a hundred pounds, could break a stack of as many as ten bricks with one slap of his palm. But it was not this technique alone that brought Pak Sing fame. His more extraordinary talent was his great control over his iron palm. He could strike the stack of bricks and break one brick in any position in the pile (that is, for example, the seventh one down) without damaging any of the others.

Another extraordinary man was Master Chin Lip Mon, a direct disciple of the famed Chin Jing, master of the *jing kuen pai* style. Chin Lip Mon was reknowned for his ability with the iron palm and with *dim mak*, a system of striking to the vital points of the body. He was also known for his tendency to drink a little more than he could handle.

Once, in such a drunken state, he wandered into the woods to take a nap, ignoring his neighbors' warnings about the tiger that had been roaming the area killing villagers. Finding a soft spot in the woods, Master Chin quickly fell asleep, only to be awakened with a start just as the dangerous tiger was about to attack. He tried to run, but when the tiger pursued, he was forced to fight bare-handed. After a long struggle in which he used his iron palm and dim mak techniques, he slew the tiger.

Chin Lip Mon, now quite sobered up, returned to the village, shouting that he had just killed the tiger. The villagers were annoyed at being awakened by this drunken man with wild stories. In the morning, however, when the workers went about their daily chores, they discovered the dead tiger in the woods. They apologized to Chin Lip Mon, and soon made him the village hero, calling him Tiger Master of jing kuen pai. Soon after, he established a school in the village and spread his art.

More advanced than iron palm training is ch'i training. The Chinese character *ch'i*, like most Chinese characters, has more than one meaning. Ch'i means, for example, "air." It is also the "life force," or "breath" of all living beings. Like electricity, or even the wind, ch'i is a force that exists and can be felt, even though it has no color, no smell, and no shape. The effects of electricity or the wind or ch'i can sometimes be seen,

Master breaking seventh brick with iron palm.

but the force itself cannot. One can see a tree being blown over by the wind, but one cannot see the wind itself.

Ch'i is so essential to the functioning of the human body that it is, in fact, the basis for traditional Chinese medicine. Explained very simply, ch'i flows throughout every person's body along certain pathways. These pathways are called *meridians.* In some ways, ch'i and meridians are like electricity and circuits. When electrical circuits are clear and electricity flows easily, an electrical system will work well. If a short circuit occurs, or wires become disconnected or broken, then the electrical system will fail—lights will go off, motors will stop. In a similar way, if the ch'i flow along meridians in the body is interrupted or in some disorder, illness or disease will result. Just as an electrician or mechanic sets to work repairing a broken electrical circuit, so too a Chinese doctor sets to work regulating and repairing the ch'i flow.

The ancient and "mysterious" Chinese medical practice called *acupuncture*, which has just recently caught the attention of Western medicine, is based on these same concepts. Acupuncture is an art which uses needles inserted into specific points of the body to regulate ch'i flow and make people healthy again.

Western thinking has not fully recognized the existence of ch'i, even though there are many well-known examples of its operation. Familiar stories are told of the mother who miraculously lifts up an automobile to save her child trapped beneath it. Her extraordinary strength comes from her use of ch'i. When people lift very heavy objects, they unconsciously breathe in and hold their breath. If they exhaled instead, they would find it very difficult to lift that same object. This feeling of extra strength comes from the operation of ch'i.

Even though all people have ch'i, in most cases it is untapped, undeveloped, and uncontrolled. While the woman tapped her ch'i potential under extreme stress, she would probably not have been able to do so in a calm, rational moment. In kung fu, however, ch'i is recognized as the practitioners' primary source of energy, and they consciously train to develop or cultivate their ch'i. They do special exercises so they can have a smooth, good ch'i flow and can control and use ch'i at will. Said another way, they learn to keep their circuits in good condition and to channel their energy so that their bodies can become more efficient, powerful motors.

The primary exercise for cultivating ch'i is called *meditation*. It is done by practicing special breathing exercises while sitting, lying, or standing in certain body positions. Meditation requires that the body be in proper posture and alignment so that the meridians in the body are free and not blocking each other. A beginning ch'i development posture, for example, is to sit on a chair with back and head in a straight line, thighs parallel to the ground, and knees and lower legs at right angles to the thighs. Hands are on the knees. This is very simple to do, and everyone can try it. From this position, students are taught special ways to breathe, and at the same time, they meditate—that is, they think deeply and concentrate on their breathing.

At advanced levels kung fu practitioners learn more and more difficult positions and breathing patterns, and eventually, after much practice, they can actually begin to feel the ch'i pulsate in their bodies, and can begin to gain control over it.

In contrast to the West, where the younger athlete is most respected, in the East it is the older master who receives this respect. Muscular strength tends to pass with youth, but ch'i strength increases with age, and with ch'i strength comes more energy and better fighting technique.

Practicing these increasingly difficult exercises for many years leads to the development of what is called *nai gung*, or "inner strength." Said another way, people who have nai gung have gained control of their ch'i, and those few who have done so can perform many miraculous feats. Masters can be so powerful they can do what is called *extending* their ch'i. This means they can point a finger in the direction of an opponent, concentrate on sending their own body's ch'i outward toward the other person, and almost like the wind, knock down the opponent with this invisible force. Some masters are so internally strong, they can take enormous blows to the body. Master Wai Fok, for example, could take a full kick in the stomach from a horse without any ill effect.

Through the development of nai gung, masters can also make their bodies extremely light or heavy. Master Chan Mon Cheung, head of the *Jow ga* system, demonstrates his lightness by performing fighting techniques while balanced on delicate tea cups. In the old days, masters who had developed what is known as *hee gung*, a type of nai gung, were so light and could jump so high they almost seemed to be flying. On the other hand, Master Chin Jing, a very small man who weighed no more than ninety pounds, could become so heavy that at one demonstration, five two-hundred-pound students could not lift him from the ground.

Aside from these quite miraculous feats, ch'i has served as the great equalizer in the martial arts. Regardless of weight, height, or muscles, it is the person who has developed ch'i and knows how to use it correctly who is victorious in a match. The number of famous women martial artists in Chinese history can be attributed largely to ch'i development, for women's reliance upon internal power compensated for their generally smaller stature, making them equal matches for any person. In fact, out of necessity—unable to rely entirely on muscle power—women often developed ch'i faster than the male students.

Considering all the above, it is no wonder that methods of ch'i development have always been some of the most closely guarded secrets of the Chinese martial arts.

MEDICAL TRAINING

In the Western world people visit doctors when they get sick, but in China people usually go to the doctor in order *not* to get sick. They get a checkup to prevent future illness. This is called *preventive medicine*, and has been a tradition in China for centuries. Since Bodhidarma's introduction of health and strengthening

A master who has developed nai gung demonstrates his lightness by balancing on delicate teacups.

exercises for the monks of Shaolin, people have also taken up kung fu as a kind of preventive medicine—to keep themselves fit. Even today it is primarily for health purposes that thousands of people in Hong Kong, Taiwan, and The People's Republic of China get up before dawn every day, make their way to local parks and, as the sun rises, do various kung fu sets before they go off to work.

With this close tie between kung fu and good health, it is not at all surprising to find that throughout China's history the majority of kung fu masters have also been physicians, and regular kung fu training involves learning traditional Chinese healing techniques along with punches and kicks.

According to legend, an old Chinese wise man who was gifted with a transparent belly experimented with eating natural plants and herbs to discover exactly what effect they would have on his body. In line with this tradition, the Chinese have developed over the centuries a comprehensive system of herbal medicine—considered ludicrous by the West until recent experiments proved that traditional ancient Chinese medicines contain natural curative vitamins and minerals.

Kung fu students learn how to apply herbal medicines to those inevitable bruises and black eyes, as well as how to set broken bones and use acupuncture for healing injuries. They are also taught resuscitation techniques, such as how to slap a special area on the soles of the feet to revive someone who has been knocked unconscious.

Knowing how to hurt without knowing how to heal would make kung fu a most incomplete system.

STYLES

At various times in Chinese history people have studied the movements of animals in the hopes of finding the key to better health and a longer life. As long ago as the third century A.D., a brilliant surgeon named Hua T'o (A.D. 190–265) developed a series of exercises for health based on the movements of the deer, tiger, bear, monkey, and bird. Since that time many others, and especially martial artists, have turned to animals in their search for a key to better, more efficient movement.

According to legend, about three hundred years ago there lived a young Shaolin monk named Wong Long whose martial arts skills were, unfortunately, quite mediocre. His teacher, about to embark upon a three-year pilgrimage, expressed hope that Wong Long's fighting technique would be markedly improved when he returned.

During the following months Wong Long gave serious thought to improving his fighting skills and one day, while walking through the woods, he noticed a fight between two insects, a praying mantis and a locust. Intrigued by the mantis' successful defense, he took the insect home with him, probed it carefully with a stick, studied its movements, and gradually began to incorporate the mantis' techniques into his own fighting style. When the senior monk returned from his lengthy jour-

Praying Mantis system of kung fu: mantis hand movements and monkey footwork.

ney, he was so impressed by Wong Long's new techniques that he took him on as his special student. The older monk found Wong Long's mantis hand movements excellent, but felt that the footwork might be improved by the addition of strong and agile foot techniques patterned after monkey movements. In this manner the two worked together, and after a few years developed a very refined fighting style called the Praying Mantis System. Today Praying Mantis is one of the most popular kung fu styles in China.

Another story tells of the famous Shaolin monk whose specialty in fighting was known as the Tiger Claw system. One day this monk attempted to rid the temple garden of a huge white crane that had come to munch on the vegetables. Although he picked up a large stick and swung it to scare the crane away, the bird

quickly raised one leg and easily avoided the strike. As hard as the monk tried to chase the crane away, the elusive, graceful body movements of this bird avoided all his efforts. Later, when the monk had some time to reflect, he thought about his encounter with the crane and began to formulate a series of graceful, fluid movements in imitation of the crane motions. He blended these movements into his own system, the Tiger Claw, and what evolved was called the Tiger-Crane kung fu system.

This system might have remained known to only a few had it not been for a man named Wong Fei Wong, a Tiger-Crane master of later years. Wong, an excellent bone doctor and herbalist, was also the Chinese Robin Hood of his day, helping villagers fight against the local landlords who took all their money, and the marauding bandits who continually terrorized them. It was his fame as a fighter for justice that spread knowledge of his Tiger-Crane style throughout China, making it the popular style it is today.

It was not just wonderful animal movements that influenced kung fu masters in the development of style. Some movements were shaped, for example, by the areas where people lived. The Hung style, named after its original founder Master Yuen Hung, developed in the southern coastal regions of China where people made their living from the sea and had to protect themselves from the pirates that sailed the waters at that time. In creating a fighting style that could be used in a boat, they found it advantageous to use rooted, low-leg positions rather than intricate kicks, and to rely more heavily upon hand movements. To this day the Hung style, popular in southern China, is characterized by very low stances and strong hand movements.

In contrast, some of the northern styles such as Praying Mantis, the Eagle Claw system, and *t'ai chi ch'uan* were developed in the mountainous regions of China where there was much snow, ice, and uneven ground. Because the area was not suitable for holding a firm, rooted stance, the styles that developed were often based more upon agility of movement and were characterized by much rolling, kicking, and jumping. Heavy winter garments hindered the development of intricate hand movements.

Of course it was individual women and men who created these various styles, and inevitably it was their personal needs that influenced the techniques they created. One famous master, Ng Mui, developed her own style to fit her particular body type.

According to legend, some three hundred years ago, during the Ch'ing Dynasty, Ng Mui was a Buddhist nun in a Shaolin monastery in southern China. She had studied several of the animal styles and found them unsuitable for her. After analyzing her own body's strengths and weaknesses and making changes and refinements from the styles she already knew, she gradually developed her own distinct style. She felt, for example, that because her arms were not particularly strong and her body was quite small, she could not do very effective punches to the midsection of a large, powerful man. She therefore began to emphasize strikes to the head and kicks to the lower legs of the opponent—two more vulnerable areas. These approaches then became an integral part of her new and very aggressive style.

As was the tradition, Ng Mui went out and challenged many of the masters of the day. She won many of her matches, thereby legitimizing her style. Ng Mui's ideas were so good, in fact, that many other kung fu styles began to imitate hers, and she became quite famous in her time.

One day Ng Mui took as her student a young woman named Yim Wing Chun. (The name means "beautiful springtime.") She taught her all she knew, and after Ng Mui died, Yim Wing Chun carried on her style. In time this system, which had no name, became known as Wing Chun kung fu.

While Wing Chun was originally known as a

women's style, in later years it was studied by many men as well. Some famous masters came from this system, including Yip Man who popularized it in Hong Kong, and his student, Bruce Lee, who introduced Wing Chun to the West, making it internationally famous. In recent years, many women studying kung fu have chosen the Wing Chun style because they are proud of its female origins.

As a further distinction among styles, there is much talk of "hard" or "external" systems, and "soft" or "internal" systems. Hard or external usually refers to the use of the body's external muscular force, while soft or internal refers to the use of technique and internal forces such as ch'i. Many Westerners, prone to labeling and categorizing, have tried to place all kung fu styles in one or the other category, yet the Chinese do not separate their systems in this way.

The master of kung fu seeks balance—balance of the self, balance with society, with nature, with the universe. The ideal state in kung fu is to be neither hard nor soft, but to be both hard and soft. It is to be like water.

Water is soft. It flows and will take any shape. If you press down on a pool of water, the water will give way to the hand. Yet if you have ever been hit by a wave at the beach, you know the tremendous power of water.

In kung fu one punches and kicks in both a hard and soft manner, much as a towel can be snapped. A towel by itself is loose, limp, and soft, yet if it is snapped quickly, like a whip, it becomes powerful and is rigid and hard at the moment of contact.

This duality of hard and soft is based on the Chinese

Wing Chun, originated by a woman and introduced to the West by Bruce Lee.

concept of *yin and yang.* This philosophy holds that all things in the world are made up of opposites which work in harmony, complementing each other. Day and night are opposites, but they work together. There can be no day without night, no night without day. In the same way, there can be no hard without soft, no soft without hard.

Still other kung fu styles were developed from the various philosophical trends that had existed in China for centuries. T'ai chi ch'uan (The Supreme Ultimate Fist), an art which will be discussed in a later chapter, developed from the yin/yang and Taoist schools of thought.

There are indeed hundreds of styles of kung fu in China, too numerous to list. Some of the more popular styles are *bak mei* (White Eyebrow), *hsing-yi* (Mind Form), *Hung ga* (Hung Family System), Jow ga (Jow Family System), and jing kuen pai (The Righteous Fist). One of the most recent styles, and evidence of the fact that new systems are forever being developed, is Bruce Lee's style, *jeet kune do* (The Way of the Intercepting Fist). This style came primarily from Wing Chun and was still in the developmental stage when Bruce Lee died in 1973.

No one kung fu style should be considered superior to any other. Some people are tall, some short, others fat, and still others thin, so everyone's body will move differently. A style suited to one person's body might not be suitable for another. It is therefore advisable to seek a good teacher who may be able to tell you what style would be best for you.

All kung fu styles have the same goal, just different means of attaining it. While many people today study kung fu for physical health or self-defense purposes, the highest goal of all kung fu study is to obtain unity of one's physical, mental, and spiritual selves. Said another way, kung fu is directed toward the full discovery and use of a human being's full potential—a potential that is barely tapped during the average person's lifetime.

If one understands these principles, it is not surprising to find that some of the great kung fu masters were highly accomplished in many areas of life other than the martial arts. Cheng Man Ch'ing, a t'ai chi ch'uan master who taught in New York City until his death in 1975, epitomizes the fully developed kung fu master. He was known in China as "The Five Treasures of Taiwan" for his expertise in calligraphy, painting, poetry, medicine, and t'ai chi ch'uan.

As the word *kung fu* indicates, such high attainment takes many years, but one can start to work immediately. Value can be obtained from the first five minutes of training to the ninetieth year. There is no age limit to the study of kung fu, for it involves much more than just youthful physical activity. The only limitation is your own. How much you get out of kung fu depends on you.

2 JUDO

Judo, a relatively new addition to the martial arts, has its roots in the fighting systems of feudal Japan. From the tenth until the eighteenth centuries the various provinces (similar to states) of Japan were constantly fighting each other for control of land and riches. Out of this turmoil and continual warfare a class of professional warriors, or knights, was formed, similar to the European knights of about the same time period.

These fierce Japanese warriors were called *samurai*. They were highly skilled fighters who battled marvelously with bows and arrows, swords, spears, and other weapons. They usually rode on horseback and wore armor, enormous helmets, and metal masks that were made to look like their real faces so they could be recognized in battle. Sometimes the men even added false mustaches to their masks to give them a fiercer appearance.

In the very early years of Japanese history, Japanese women had been warrior queens who ruled lands and led troops in battle. During this feudal period, however, men had taken power from them, and most women were kept off the battlefield. There were still some samurai women who hadn't given up their power, and they continued to fight skillfully alongside or even in command of the men. Two such women, Itagaki and Tomoe, will be discussed in the chapter on *naginata*. All samurai women were trained in the use of weapons,

42

Tomoe Gozen Killing Uchido Saburo Ieyoshi. *By Toyonobu, c.1750.*

especially spears and small daggers, and were expected to be courageous and skilled fighters in defending their homes, or in assuming command in the event of a husband's death.

All the many ways of fighting that these samurai men and women practiced—and they knew a great many— were called *bujutsu. Bu* means "military" or "fighting," *jutsu* means "arts," so *bujutsu,* just like the Chinese term wu su, means "military" or "fighting arts."

All samurai women and men followed a code similar to the code of chivalry of the European knights. They were supposed to be brave and honorable in the cause of justice, and act with politeness and even gracefulness at all times. For all their fierceness in battle, they had special ideas of fair play. It was very important that a samurai fight another warrior who was an equally good

43

fighter. Before a battle, the samurai would ride up on horseback to the enemy, and announce loudly and fiercely who they were, who their ancestors were, what battles they had fought and won, and other information they thought important. In this way they not only made themselves feel more courageous, but also ensured that only an enemy of "equal" qualifications would fight them. There are even stories of samurai refusing to kill enemies because they were too young or too inexperienced as fighters.

At certain periods in Japanese history these warriors were even expected to learn music, poetry, and flower arranging, to make them have more gentleness and good feeling for others. Samurai enemies sometimes recited poetry to each other on the battlefield, trying to outdo one another by composing the most clever or most beautiful poem on the spot. One great hero, named Ota Dokan, while dying with a spear in his side, is said to have composed perfect final lines to a poem his enemy had begun. Calmness in the face of death was considered a great samurai virtue.

While much of this seems strange to us today, and it is highly unlikely that we would recite poetry in the midst of battle, the spirit and feeling of this warrior code, called *bushido*, or "military knight ways," have always been highly revered by the Japanese and have been preserved in the martial arts that have come down to us today.

The samurai knew many different ways to fight. On the battlefield they liked most of all to fight with their swords, or with their bows and arrows when they were

 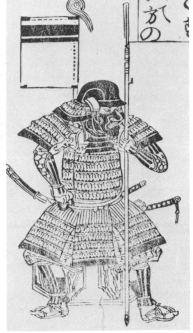

Woman samurai from Women of Military Prowess, *1766. By Tsukioka (Settei).*

Illustration by Murai from A Single Horseman: Summary of How to Wear Armor, *1735.*

far away from their enemy. Occasionally something happened to prevent this, and they had to be prepared with other techniques. A warrior might be knocked off his horse during a fight on the battlefield, and perhaps even lose a sword on the way down. If this happened, he had to be ready to fight in some other way. For this reason, warriors studied various ways of fighting on the battlefield without any weapons at all, or with only small weapons such as daggers.

They learned, for example, an art called *kumiuchi*, which was how to throw down an opponent and wrestle on the ground. They studied *atemi*, or how to strike at vital areas of the body with their bare hands so they could knock out an enemy with a single blow. They learned how to pull other warriors off their horses, and they practiced how to kick, choke, and lock and break joints in various parts of the body. All these battlefield techniques were designed to do in one's enemy in any way possible, with no holds barred.

The Japanese themselves invented many of these special fighting ways, but they were also influenced by the kung fu of China. According to legend, a Chinese poet, scholar, and Ming Dynasty general, Chen Yuan-pin (called Gempin in Japan), took a great deal of martial-arts information to Japan when he hurried there in the 1600's to escape the Manchus, who had placed a price on his head. Chen traveled around Japan, and one day while visiting a Japanese temple he met three wandering samurai. Chen, a knowledgeable martial artist, is said to have taught these men techniques of throwing, punching, and joint locking. After much study the three samurai went their separate ways, opening three different martial-arts schools based upon these new teachings of Chen.

Another story tells of Skiyama Shorobei, a Japanese doctor, who while traveling and studying in China during this same period learned an art called *hakuda*. When he later returned to Japan he took with him the kicking and striking specialties of this art, enhancing the already-expanding Japanese martial arts.

These varied and quite deadly arts, while called by many different names, such as kumiuchi and hakuda, all came to be called by the overall name of *jujutsu* (some-

46

A fighter trained in the martial arts could often overpower an armed opponent.

times written *jujitsu* or *jiujitsu*). Like the term kung fu, jujutsu refers not to one, but to all these various unarmed and small-arms fighting methods.

While hundreds of jujutsu systems had existed over the centuries, it was not until the 1700's and early 1800's that jujutsu really flourished. Strangely, this golden age of jujutsu was brought about not because people were fighting more and more, but rather because, after centuries of warfare, a period of peace actually came to Japan. People were fighting less and less.

Overnight the startled samurai had become warriors without a war to fight. They were similar to the gunfighters of the American West, who once ruled the land with their guns until the West became "civilized" and "shoot-em-ups" were no longer the way to decide all disputes. Just as some of the "fastest guns" in the West probably slowed down when they were out of practice, so too, many samurai warriors, long out of practice, were poor with the sword. Some no longer knew how to hold their swords, much less how to use them. In general, without practical use for these war arts, many bujutsu were in decline, and some were beginning to disappear altogether. Many samurai, feeling a lack of purpose in life, took to hanging around teahouses drinking all day, and some even drifted to lives of crime.

Given this situation, it is no wonder that it was now sometimes possible for a skilled, knowledgeable jujutsu practitioner to actually disarm and successfully fight such a sword wielder, whereas before, those trained in the sword were most often the better fighters. Jujutsu also became more feasible now that samurai warriors no longer wore all that bulky wartime armor. It had sometimes been necessary in the past to wrestle or punch and kick such an armored person, but it had certainly never been easy.

Stories about jujutsu spread around the country. It was said that one day in a small tavern on the outskirts of Tokyo, a huge ugly man wearing the two swords that were the traditional mark of a samurai was making a lot of noise and insulting all the customers. The owner of the shop, a meek-looking person, approached to calm down the samurai, who had definitely had a little too much *sake* to drink. The warrior, seeing the size of this small proprietor, began to bully him. He went to grab him, but the tavern owner easily slipped from his grip. The huge samurai was quite surprised, and couldn't figure out how the man had done this. He became furious, and as tipsy as he was, he went to draw his sword, whereupon the owner grabbed his arm, twisted it, and threw the samurai over his shoulder—his sword and his heavy body crashing to the floor with a loud clank and thud. The other customers were amazed to see the weaponless tavern owner subdue the heavily armed samurai. "What techniques are you using?" the people asked. "Why," replied the tavern owner, "jujutsu, of course."

As such tales spread, so did the popularity of the jujutsu arts. More and more people approached the jujutsu masters, asking to become their students. Jujutsu schools flourished, and people everywhere took up these lively arts. There were hundreds of different schools, with some stressing grappling, others punching and kicking, and others still different techniques.

JIGARO KANO AND THE FOUNDING OF JUDO

Into this exciting period, on October 28, 1860, a boy by the name of Jigaro Kano was born. He was to profoundly influence the future of jujutsu.

As a child, Kano was weak and sickly, and because of this, bullies were always picking on him and beating him up. Kano decided to take up sports and become strong. He played baseball and gymnastics and went rowing and hiking. Gradually he developed some muscles and some strength, and was definitely in better shape. While a college student of eighteen, Kano became interested in jujutsu and decided to try it out. At a jujutsu school under the direction of Hachinosuke Fukuda and a Mr. Iso, Kano began his studies. The jujutsu emphasized in this school consisted of striking techniques, called *atemi-waza*, and grappling techniques, *katame-waza.*

This young boy fell in love with jujutsu. He trained harder and longer than the other students, and it was difficult to send him home at day's end. He trained constantly, even though practice in this art was very rough. His training jacket was torn to shreds, and his body was always black and blue. Kano tried to care for his injuries himself, and he spread his own medicine on his bruises. His friends teased him and complained that the medicine smelled so bad that they knew Kano was coming even before they could see him.

When both of Kano's teachers died, he studied at another jujutsu school under an instructor named Iikubo. This school specialized in *nage-waza*, or throwing techniques, and in places where Kano hadn't gotten bruises before, he certainly got them now.

But Jigaro Kano was not easily discouraged. The more he learned about jujutsu, the more he wanted to know. He began to read everything he could about the arts, spent time in libraries, and talked to all the jujutsu masters he could find.

In time, Kano grew disturbed, for he realized that the arts of jujutsu, like many of the other samurai fighting arts, were gradually disintegrating. Historical events were having their effect. In the 1860's and 1870's, the feudal Tokugawa regime that ruled Japan was overthrown, and feudal ways were now considered old-fashioned. Even the special rights of the samurai class were taken away. Most Japanese wanted to modernize quickly, to do away with many of the old ways.

As one might imagine, the effect on the martial arts—an old-time, feudal institution—was close to disastrous. Many jujutsu students quit their training and stopped coming to class. Jujutsu teachers, many of whom were out of work with little or no money, were sometimes forced into doing things they would never have done before. Some put on shows of strength and fighting for money, others took challenges from people in the other arts and charged admission. Many became bullies and rowdies. Most were unhappy.

Other arts suffered as well, and the plight of women in the arts was especially sad. Without a class of women samurai, women's martial arts all but disappeared, for it was considered scandalous for a woman from a non-military family to train alongside men in martial-arts schools. If any training went on, it was done very privately.

Kano loved jujutsu so much that he became determined to save it and bring it back to the wonderful art it had once been. He set up his own school in a tiny room in a Tokyo temple where he was living. Kano called his new school *Kodokan judo.*

Jujutsu to Judo

Kodokan means "the place for studying the way." It was Kano's choice of the word *judo* rather than *jujutsu,* however, that was most important. First, he wanted a name that would set him apart from the other jujutsu schools that had recently developed such bad reputations.

Second, by keeping the *ju* (flexibility) from *ju-jutsu* (the art of flexibility), but changing the ending to *do* (*ju-do*, the way of flexibility), Kano was in fact reflecting a trend that was taking place all over Japan. Many of the masters of the other martial arts—the older bujutsu teachers—had begun to create new variations on the old arts. They developed arts that would be more up-to-date and appealing to the people of the time, yet would still develop brave, strong, disciplined martial artists who felt good about themselves as the old-time warriors had.

They called their new arts *budo,* meaning "military way," instead of the older bujutsu, or "military art." Whereas bujutsu training was mainly for practical purposes—to teach warriors how to survive a rough day on the battlefield, or to teach modern town officials how to deal with local ruffians—peacetime budo training was done primarily for character development. Training in budo was open to all classes of people, not only samurai. Budo was designed to create in each of its practitioners a beautiful personality that would survive well in the everyday world and even contribute to the betterment of society. Similarly to kung fu, budo trained one to attain spiritual enlightenment as well as mental and physical fitness. Said another way, bujutsu training was geared for competition against one's enemy, while budo training was aimed at competing against oneself, striving for greater and greater self-perfection.

Individual martial arts that changed from the old bujutsu style to the new budo style often changed the endings of their names from *jutsu* to *do.* It is understandable now why Kano changed *jujutsu* to *judo*, for he too wanted his favorite martial art to change in the same way that the other bujutsu were changing—away from the feeling of the battlefield, and more toward what he called the "mutual welfare and benefit" of its practitioners.

Another reason Kano changed was that jujutsu, like the other old-style jutsu arts, was a very dangerous activity, whereas the budo systems were milder. In these *do* arts, fighting was more a mock battle, and while a person missing a block might end up with a sizeable lump on the head, this was nothing compared to the bujutsu practice, where a person missing the same block might end up with no head at all. While the jutsu arts trainees were exceptionally tough, they sometimes did not live too long.

It is silly, said Kano, for training to be so dangerous, especially in peacetime. When people work out with their friends, there is no need to throw them with the hope of hurting them. To do this means, first, they will have no one to practice with the next day, and second, they certainly won't have a friend anymore. Wouldn't it be much better, he reasoned, if people could practice judo so that at the end of the day everyone was still standing, feeling good, liking each other, and ready to come back the next day to work out together again?

To encourage this, Kano decided all students had to wear a special uniform called a *gi*—a thick quilted white jacket and loose pajamalike pants. This, of course, was a good idea, since if a person wore regular clothes for workout, they would get torn and stretched. But more than this, Kano required that the person throwing a partner must grip the falling person's uniform and control the speed and position of the fall, not letting the opponent land with full force. For the first time, throwers were responsible for the safety of their opponents.

Next, to further help prevent cracked heads and such, Kano decided to spend part of each class teaching people how to fall correctly so they wouldn't get hurt.

Following the traditions of bushido, Kano also expected students to use fair play with each other. This meant that a skilled old-timer was not supposed to totally defeat a new beginner. The spirit of the art had so changed from wartime jujutsu that now when one did judo, one called it "playing" judo rather than "fighting."

Kano saw judo primarily as a means for becoming a better person who would then help improve society. He felt so strongly about this that he said if a judo player "does not benefit society, his [or her] existence is in vain."

Jujutsu had changed a great deal from the past, and the meaning of the *do* in judo is quite clear.

The Concept of Ju

Ju, the first part of the word *judo*, means "yielding," "flexible," "pliable," "adaptable." In the martial arts it refers to the idea of giving way to gain an advantage. *Jujutsu* can be translated as "the art of flexibility" and judo as "the way of flexibility" or "the way of yielding." While some people even prefer to call judo "the gentle way," this does not imply weakness, but rather a way to survive and win.

Kano kept the *ju* in his new name, for *ju* expressed the way in which both jujutsu and judo worked—a way he liked and wanted to develop. The concept of ju had long been used by other Japanese arts, and had originated with the kung fu of China. The concept stems from the Taoist philosophies of yin and yang, the "unity of opposites," that was mentioned earlier. It is expressed best by the Chinese philosopher Lao-tze, who said, "The most yielding things in the world master the most unyielding," and "A branch of a tree that bends in the storm will survive. A stiff branch will break."

Applied to the practice of judo or jujutsu, *ju* means that when you fight you do not pit your strength head-on against the strength of your opponent. If a truck were bearing down on you on the street, it would be ridiculous to try to stop it by standing in front of it, trying to push it away. To survive, you would step out of the way, yield, as fast as possible. This is proper use of ju.

Similarly, if a very strong person pushes against you, and you push back head-on with your own weaker strength, you will certainly be defeated. If instead you step back and give way in the direction your opponent is pushing, and in addition pull the opponent in the direction he or she is already pushing, you can actually throw your opponent down very hard. In this application of ju, you use the opponent's strength against him or her. You now have two strengths working for you instead of one—your opponent's strength in pushing you and your own strength in pulling them.

As an old Taoist saying goes, "When opponents come, welcome them; when they go, send them on their way." To Kano, using ju was the way to make "the best use of energy," and "the maximum efficient use of mind and body." These principles, more than any others,

56

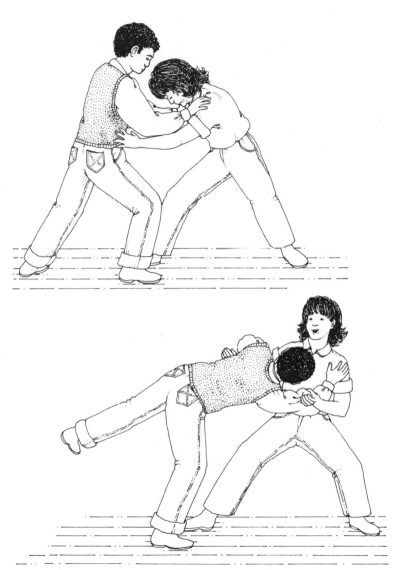

An illustration of pushing and pulling in judo.

expressed what judo meant. He believed these principles should not be used only in judo practice, but that one should make the maximum efficient use of one's mind and body in one's whole life, or else one will not be living in the right way.

Scientific Principles, Not Magic

In addition to the principle of ju, Kano paid particular attention to the science of physics. Every technique that Kano decided to use in his system had to work on clear scientific principles, such as leverage and gravity.

Kano's approach was quite new, for many schools and people before him had stressed the mysteries and secrets of jujutsu, perpetuating ideas that the various arts were done mostly by magic.

The scientific basis of judo meant there was a logical way to do throws and other techniques in Kano's system. If students worked hard and followed the principles, they would be successful.

There is an often-told story that illustrates this idea. In one judo school, many years after Kano's time, the students were spending every day trying to do a particularly difficult throw. They kept pulling and tugging at each other, but no one could do the throw right. The teacher, meanwhile, made the same corrections every day. "Relax more, pull harder, and go lower," she said, time and time again. Weeks and months passed. The students tried again and again, the teacher made the same comments, and there was still no success. The students were beginning to lose hope, when finally, by what looked like magic, one of the students did the throw perfectly, cleanly, and with apparent great ease. All the students rushed over to her and asked excitedly, "How did you do it? Tell us, tell us, what is the secret?" The student thought, analyzing carefully exactly what she had done so she could explain it. "First, I really relaxed, then I pulled very hard, and then I went really low."

Good technique in judo does not come by chance, luck, or magic, but by following correct principles and practicing them over and over again. A Japanese judo teacher, Shiro Oishi of New York City, says, "My advice to children is, if you want to be good at it, you have to spend time. That's the important thing. If a person sticks to judo long enough, and concentrates hard, then that person will eventually know judo and know themselves as well." Kano himself is reputed to have said that the secret of judo could be stated in three words: "Never Miss Practice."

Kano's Worldwide System

With his two principles, mutual benefit and the best use of energy, clearly in mind, plus his concept of ju, his idea of *do*, and his scientific principles, Kano proceeded over the next several years to set up his own martial-arts system. He took a good look at the different jujutsu moves he had studied, selected the ones that fit his ideas and principles, eliminated all those that didn't, and modified others that were too dangerous. He developed one comprehensive lesson plan for teaching judo, and wrote everything down so it would be easy for people everywhere to follow his plan.

While many people liked Kano's new ideas, they weren't so sure that his students could hold up in a match. Just a lot of words, they thought. No action. Kano had a chance to prove himself in 1886 when the Tokyo Police Department held a tournament between Kano's school and another jujutsu school called Yoshin Ryu. The two schools sent fifteen students each to fight in the tournament. To the surprise of many the Kodokan won easily, taking almost all the matches, proving that Kano's principles also developed fine fighters.

As years went by Kano's judo became one of the most popular martial arts in Japan. In 1890, even children in the public schools began to play judo. In 1911, judo became compulsory for boys in all middle schools, and in time judo was practiced in all the government universities and military schools of Japan.

More and more women also wanted the chance to enjoy judo. In 1893, eleven years after Kano founded the Kodokan, a woman named Sueko Ashiya came to him, asking for lessons. He accepted her as his first woman student, and soon after Kano began teaching judo to his wife, his daughter, and their friends in his own home. One woman, Kinko Yasuda, lived with the Kano family so she could practice there every day.

Women finally progressed out of this living-room-training situation when Kano opened the *joshi-bu*, or women's section, of the Kodokan in the mid-1920's. Keiko Fukuda, the granddaughter of Hachinosuke Fukuda, one of Kano's first jujutsu teachers, was one of the first women to study there. Kano invited her to train with him, and at twenty-one years of age she began to do so.

Fukuda, "judo's oldest student," as she likes to call herself, remembers that like most Japanese girls she had studied tea ceremony, flower arranging, and calligraphy, but because of her grandfather, she had always felt a pull toward judo. Her family encouraged her, to a point. Says Fukuda, "My mother's and brother's thoughts were for me to learn, and get married to a *judoka* [a judo player] someday, but not to become a judoka myself. After I joined the Kodokan, judo became the most important part of my life."

Many women, most with probably quite similar stories, since judo for women was not quite the proper thing to do, began training with Keiko Fukuda at the joshi-bu, and little by little, the women's section grew. The students loved training, and many of the women excelled. Kano is reputed to have often told his men judoka, "If you really want to know true judo, take a look at the methods they use at the Kodokan joshi-bu."

Despite this high praise, and the changing times, Japanese women today are still training only in the women's section of the Kodokan, and except for very special situations are not allowed to train with the men.

Kano was very happy with the success of judo in Japan, but even more, he thought if he could spread judo throughout the world, people everywhere would learn to overcome their differences and be more caring toward each other. To achieve this, Kano spent much of his later life traveling around the world to spread his ideas. One of his aims was to get judo accepted as a sport for Olympic competition. When Kano died, in 1938, he was on a Japanese steamer on his way home from an International Olympic Committee meeting in Egypt. While he did not live to see his dream come true, judo was finally accepted in the Olympics of 1964.

From Kano's original nine students, the number of judoka all over the world expanded into millions. In 1879, Keiko Fukuda's grandfather and Kano performed a demonstration for former United States President Ulysses S. Grant, who was visiting Japan. And a few years later, President of the United States Theodore Roosevelt, an athletic, vigorous person who had done boxing and wrestling for many years, took up judo. He invited Kano's students, Yoshiaki Yamashita, a tenth-degree black belt, and Fudeko Yamashita, husband and wife, to come to the United States. In the early 1900's, these two judoka taught Roosevelt and his son in the White House. Sometimes when people came on business to see Teddy Roosevelt, he would practice his judo techniques with them, and even forget to discuss the official business.

It was not only Kano's judo but other jujutsu systems as well that spread throughout the world during this period. From 1913 to 1914, the suffragists in England—women who were involved in fights with the police in their attempts to secure the right to vote for women—decided to learn how to protect themselves. They found a jujutsu school and signed up immediately. These militant suffragists proceeded to learn jujutsu and then formed a group called the Bodyguard. More and more women joined, and most did so secretly, like the two sisters from a prominent British family who sneaked out each night to join the Bodyguard by climbing down the drainpipe of their house.

Members of the Bodyguard were skilled and courageous, sometimes successfully fighting off the police who tried to prevent them from giving speeches to the public. While many of the Bodyguard were injured and arrested during this tumultuous period, none ever quit. According to Nell Hall Humpherson, a feminist of that period, "Nobody ever left the Bodyguard. Nobody ever resigned from the Bodyguard. We just got more people."

While there were undoubtedly many such exciting uses of jujutsu during this period of history, it was largely because of Kano's efforts—his excellent lesson plan and his promotion of the art—that his special revision of jujutsu, judo, is played all over the world today, and that in such disparate places as the United States and Japan, it is practiced in very much the same manner. There are not many different styles of judo, as there are many different styles of kung fu.

TRAINING

The place where students practice is called a *dojo*. The *do* is the same *do* discussed before, meaning "the way," while *jo* means "place." Similarly to the word *Kodokan*, *dojo* means "a place for learning the way." It is the

THE SUFFRAGETTE THAT KNEW JIU-JITSU.
THE ARREST.

From Punch, *July 6, 1910.*

name used for the training hall in most Japanese martial arts.

The floor of a judo dojo is usually covered with mats so that judo students can fall without breaking bones. While decorations are usually sparse and simple, in most dojos there is a picture of Kano hanging in a prominent place in the room.

Just as Kano intended, all students wear the heavy judo gis. This gi is rugged and can take lots of wear and tear without ripping. Gi tops are kept closed by belts that are worn around the waist. These belts come in different colors and are used to show what is called *rank*, or level of achievement.

Rank and the Black Belt

Throughout martial-arts history there have been many ways to show the skill level of students and teachers. In some Chinese monasteries, for example, monks and nuns wore different-colored robes to designate various levels of skill. In other monasteries they wore colored sashes instead. In some countries, such as Burma, practitioners wear various kinds of rings on their fingers. Yet sometimes the most respected form of rank is a certificate given to the student.

One system of rank that has gained worldwide popularity was originally developed by Kano. It is called the *kyu-dan* system. (*Kyu* means "class," *dan* means "grade.") When people talks about belts and the famous black belt, it is usually this system that they are referring to.

When students first begin to study judo they wear a white belt and have no rank at all. They are sometimes called *no kyu*. As time goes on they progress through the levels of kyu ranks, of which there are five in judo. After training for some time, they first attain fifth kyu, then later fourth kyu. At this stage they still wear white belts. The next three ranks are called third, second, and first kyu, in which students wear brown belts. After this they finally attain that long-sought-for first degree black belt, also called "first dan" or *shodan* in Japanese. (It usually takes at least three years, and often much longer, to get to this point.)

Most people outside judo think this black belt is the highest grade, the mark of an "expert" martial artist, but this is not at all true. While shodan means that the student has worked hard, and is good, this rank is only the *first* level out of a possible twelve levels of black belt. Shodan usually means that the student has learned the basics well, is a serious student, and is now ready to begin learning what judo is really all about. It is during the next ten, twenty, or thirty years, as students progress to higher and higher dan rankings, that they may be considered "experts." But in judo, as in all martial arts, there is no end to training. One can always learn more.

At these higher levels, from the first to the fifth dan, the practitioners still wear black belts. As they progress higher, from sixth to eighth dan, they can wear either a red-and-white belt or a black belt; from ninth to eleventh dan, an all-red belt or a black belt; and at twelfth dan, a double-width white belt or a black belt. This highest rank is called *shidan* (meaning master grade), and no one has ever held this rank except Kano himself. The highest rank ever given out at the Kodokan (other than Kano's) was tenth dan.

Within this system there are, of course, some variations from country to country. In the United States and throughout Europe some additional colors have been added in the kyu ranks—yellows, greens, oranges, and blues, for example.

Usually kyu and dan ranks are achieved by passing tests. While the tests are different for each rank, for most promotions one must know how to do certain techniques and certain *kata*s (to be explained later), and also win against competitors in judo contests. The rules vary sometimes with the age and sex of the participant. Children are not allowed to attain black belts until they are sixteen years old.

Some of the promotional rules and the ranking system in general discriminate against women. There was a rule in the United States, for example, that although women were allowed to wear the same color belts as men, they had to have a white stripe running down the middle of their belts if they wanted to compete in the important national judo competitions. This rule made women angry. According to Diane Pierce, a top black-belt competitor: "I am a black belt, not a 'black-and-white belt.' The stripe looks to me like the wearer is not quite a brown belt and not quite a black belt. Surely it isn't there to show that you are a woman and not a man; or is it? I feel that those of us who choose to compete . . . should wear a solid belt to show that we are one hundred percent brown belts or black belts." Another female black-belt competitor says about the stripe: "To me it has always been a mark of inferiority. It implies that you are a lesser player than the men of the same rank. This is something I don't accept."

In the past few years, largely because of the women's liberation movement, there has been much protest against this kind of treatment. Many women, including the two above, have fought in competitions wearing only white belts, refusing to wear a colored belt with a stripe in it. In 1976, primarily because of these protests, the ruling was changed and women were finally allowed to wear full-colored belts.

This does not mean that ranking problems for women

are over. Because of years of discrimination of one kind or another in the judo world, there are now very few high-ranking women. Rusty Kanokogi, a New York City woman who has been studying judo for twenty years, is now a fourth-degree black belt. (She is, incidentally, one of the few women ever allowed to train with men at the Kodokan in Japan.) There are only a half dozen women in the world who hold this rank with her. Moreover, until 1972 there was a rule at the Kodokan (Kano's original school, which still controls ranking throughout the world) that prohibited women from being promoted higher than fifth dan, while men could go as high as the twelfth. In that year women all over the world wrote letters to the Kodokan protesting, and asking them to promote Keiko Fukuda, Kano's early student. Fukuda, now one of the world's greatest women players, had received her fifth-degree black belt in 1953, almost twenty years earlier. The women won, and Fukuda, who now lives and teaches in California, became the first woman sixth dan in the world. According to a friend of hers, however, Fukuda "had to be as equal in skill and knowledge to get her sixth dan as a man who has his tenth."

Dojo Etiquette

Judoka (judo players) seem to be bowing all the time in a judo dojo. Bowing is a Japanese way of greeting similar to Western handshakes. In addition to saying hello, it often means more, and is also a sign of respect.

In a judo dojo, everyone bows before getting on the mat and also before leaving, expressing respect for the learning place.

At the start of each class, the students line up in order of their rank, then kneel down in a line with their teacher in front of them. Everyone bows first to the picture of Kano, to honor the founder of the art. Then the students bow to the teacher, who is usually addressed as *sensei*, the Japanese word for teacher.

Bowing is also done before and after working with a partner. The bow used at this time shows us the *do* aspect of judo. The two players bow to each other

Judoka bowing.

calmly, peacefully. Then they begin to "play," slamming each other onto the mat with furious expressions on their faces, choking each other, letting out loud shouts from time to time. Yet, when time is called by the sensei, the two players stand up, straighten their frightfully messed-up gis, and then calmly and respectfully bow to each other as if nothing had happened.

To the Westerner this may seem a little wierd, but to judoka it makes sense in a *do* art to fight—but not for the purpose of beating up your opponent. In judo, as in other *do* arts, the purpose of the contest is to better one's own technique. The bow says just this: "Watch out, for I'm going to do my best to smash you around, but it's done to perfect my judo and myself, not to hurt you. The second this contest is over, it is forgotten and we are still friends, and, I hope, even better friends than before."

Warm-Ups

Each class begins with warm-up exercises. While they may be boring to watch, they are very important, for even the greatest players must stretch and loosen up to keep from pulling muscles and getting other injuries. Students also do strengthening exercises like push-ups for arm muscles, and sit-ups and leg raises for stomach muscles. Sometimes they do "bridging," in which one makes one's body into a bridge in order to strengthen one's back and neck—especially important for judo.

Ukemi

In any judo class it is not strange to hear loud, thundering sounds, which one soon discovers are not caused just by bodies landing with thuds on the mat. The sounds also come from hands slapping the mat very hard just a second before the body lands. Judoka learn to do this to absorb the shock of the fall with the hands so the body doesn't take the fall's full force.

Falling practice, called *ukemi*, is usually a regular part of each class, just as Kano wished. Since students are thrown in all directions, they must learn how to fall every which way. They learn special ways to fall backward, to both sides, and to the front. These falls are called *breakfalls*, since they are breaking the fall so the student doesn't become one big black-and-blue mark. Students also study *rollouts*, another good way to avoid getting hurt.

Throwing Techniques

Students then learn throwing techniques, called *nage-waza* in Japanese. All judo throws depend, first of all, upon making one's partner lose his or her balance. No matter how big people are, how strong, how muscular, tall, or athletic, if they slip on a banana peel or some ice, they will fall down just like everybody else. Making one's opponent lose his or her balance is called *unbalancing* or *breaking balance*. A player does this by pushing or pulling a partner in various directions, trying to take the partner by surprise. At the same time, the partner is trying to unbalance the player, which makes this all doubly difficult and even more interesting.

Once the opponent is off balance, the object is then, by using some kind of throw, to get him off his feet and onto the mat. Throwing a person in judo does not mean that you throw her or him in the same way you throw a ball. It means that you try to make your opponent fall down, usually near your own feet, before your partner does the same to you. You cannot throw a person any way you want, but must use only specific kinds of throws. From a standing position you can trip your opponent with your legs or feet, roll your opponent over your hips, or throw him or her by pulling with your hands. Sometimes you can fall to the ground first, and bring the other person along with you. This is called a *sacrifice technique* because you sacrifice your own balance to succeed.

Preparatory moves for a throw.

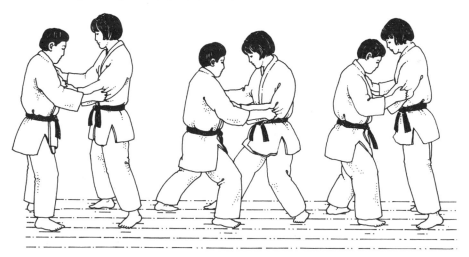

Within these categories there are many different throws, from simple to very difficult. There are also variations of throws, and you can do them with the particular style that suits your own body, in much the same way that you write the alphabet with your own distinct handwriting. Yet just as your letters must be readable, so too a specific judo throw must be recognizable as that particular throw.

One popular throw, and perhaps the easiest to learn, is called *osoto gari*, which means "big outside reap." When a judoka executes osoto gari, she or he pushes the partner backward, breaking the partner's balance to the rear. When the partner tries to step back and regain balance, the attacker steps in and hooks one leg around one of the opponent's legs, sweeping it out from under the opponent, who should then fall to the mat.

When one gets more advanced, one can do techniques such as *tomoe nage*, the throw always used in cowboy

Tomoe nage: advanced judo throwing technique.

movies. This sacrifice technique is used when your opponent moves in to attack. As he or she attacks, you step in close, grab the person by the lapels, and fall down on your back, placing one of your feet in your opponent's stomach. As you fall, you pull hard on the opponent's lapels and straighten out the leg that is planted in your opponent's stomach. As you do this, your opponent will go flying over your head and land on her or his back.

When done correctly, a throw appears to be very easy, taking little effort, but as we know, it takes much hard practice to achieve the correct timing, speed, and coordination. Against a very skilled partner it is difficult to execute any throw, let alone a good one.

There was a famous judo master, legendary in the annals of judo, called Kyuzo Mifune. He was one of the few men ever promoted to tenth dan by Kano himself. It is said that Mifune never lost a judo match. He was so difficult to throw that even when he got older and was a little white-haired old man, he couldn't be thrown. People said that trying to throw Mifune was like trying to throw a cat who always landed on all four feet. Someone once said that it was "like an elephant trying to throw a butterfly." Mifune's understanding of ju, how to gently give way and deflect attack, kept anyone from throwing him.

Mat Work: Holds, Chokes, and Locks

Once your partner is thrown onto the mat, you can

follow him or her down and apply various holds, chokes, and locks. This part is called "mat work," or *katame-waza* in Japanese. If you were to watch mat work, it might look like regular old-fashioned free-for-all wrestling that children do for fun. But there are very specific rules for mat work, just as there are for throwing, with only special techniques that can be used. (There is no poking eyes, or biting, for example.)

The object of mat work is to control your opponent's body for a certain length of time or to make the opponent give up. First, you can try to control your partner by use of a *hold-down*. There are many different holds, usually done by in some way lying on top of your opponent. One of the simplest holds is called *kesa gatame* ("scarf hold").

If you are quick enough, you can sometimes use a second kind of technique on your partner which is called a *choke*. A choke is exactly that, although it is quite different from the common fingers-around-the-throat choke we are used to seeing in movie murder mysteries. There are various methods of choking, some using your arm and others using your opponent's gi to cut off her or his air supply.

Since judo was not meant to harm its players, the choke is usually applied carefully, and when the person being choked can't escape or breathe, he or she *taps out*—taps twice with one hand, either on the mat, on his or her own body, or on the partner, to let the partner know the choke has succeeded and it's time to stop. Tapping out is an important safety measure in judo.

Without it, the mat might just be covered with the bodies of passed-out students.

Finally, a player may apply a third kind of technique from the mat, called a *lock*. These are painful, causing the opponent to surrender once more. Joints of the body such as elbow, wrist, finger, or knee bend naturally in only one direction. If you try to bend your elbow or your finger, for example, in the opposite direction, it doesn't go. If you try to force it, it really hurts. In judo locks, the person puts pressure on an elbow or shoulder to go in the direction it doesn't want to go, causing pain and submission. A common lock is called an *arm bar*. These techniques are applied very carefully. When a person is sure the opponent has a secure lock, she or he taps out.

While these chokes and locks might seem gruesome to someone who thought judo was just "fun," they really aren't. Chokes and locks are not usually used by or on beginners, and once you become experienced, you know how to apply them carefully and take them gracefully without panicking. It becomes a matter of course, and students rarely are injured from chokes or locks, even though they might pass out once or twice.

It is interesting that for every hold, choke, or lock, there is an escape, just as there is always a countermove for every throw. Students practice these as well, and can often prevent their opponents from getting good chokes or locks on them.

To prevent serious injury at times like this, Kano, like the kung fu masters, included resuscitation tech-

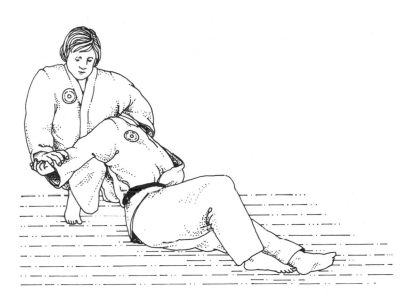

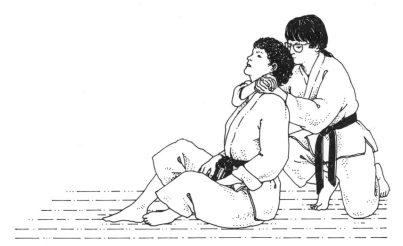

Judo arm bar lock (top); judo choke (bottom).

niques—ways of reviving an unconscious person—in his judo training. The techniques he used, called *kappo*, were developed hundreds of years before by samurai masters, and for a long time were kept as valuable secret techniques passed on only by word of mouth from master to pupil. Since Kano's time, however, these techniques have been taught more openly.

Randori

After students have learned two or three throws, can fall correctly, and know some holds and escapes, they then learn what is called *randori*, or "free play." Randori is probably the most exciting part of judo to watch, and also to do, for in it the partners are allowed to do most of the techniques they have been taught. Partners face each other, bow, and then can attempt any throw, hold, choke, or lock at any time. The object is to throw the partner down, or if they both fall to the mat, to try to hold the opponent down, preventing escape. It is randori that is done in Olympic competition.

Kata

Another important part of judo training is kata, which means "form." Katas are prearranged groups of movements, just like the sets of kung fu. Judo katas are different from kung fu sets, however, because judo katas are always done with partners, while sets are often performed alone against imaginary opponents. In a judo form there are movement patterns, one for the person who plays the role of attacker, and another for the one who defends.

In Kano's system there were several different katas—one devoted to throwing techniques, another for mat work, and some that incorporated many of the old jujutsu techniques that had been taken out of randori because they were too dangerous. In some katas people cut and thrust with daggers and swords, and strike and kick to vital points of the body. Some forms were designed to simulate fighting in heavy armor, and others have players imitate the movements of natural forces such as waves and wind. Judoka do not usually get hurt in katas because all the movements are prearranged.

Judo, like other martial arts, believes in the concept of ch'i, called *ki* in Japanese. The development of ki is much the same as in kung fu, the only difference being that many people in judo today do not strive for this development. Kano, however, was interested in ki development and encouraged his students to train for it. Practice in various katas was one of the methods recommended for developing ki.

While kata was considered by Kano to be an integral and very significant part of judo training, equal in importance to randori or contest training, many people no longer give kata the same emphasis it received in Kano's time. In some schools kata is learned for promotional tests and then not practiced again. In others it is still emphasized, particularly in women's schools. For it has been women who, often excluded from randori practice and contests in the past, have emphasized kata training and kata competition. (While women have been excluded until now from Olympic judo competition, Keiko Fukuda did perform a kata demonstration at the 1964 Olympics.)

It is unfortunate for both men and women that judo training has often been split along sexual lines, for men have had little opportunity to learn some wonderful katas, while women have often not been allowed to develop their fighting spirit in randori. The art of judo has, itself, suffered, losing much of the balanced training that Kano so wished for.

Contests

Competitions, called *shiai*, are held in which judoka compete against each other in randori. Points are scored by throwing an opponent, holding him or her down for a certain length of time, or choking or locking her or him into submission—or by a combination of all of these. Kata competitions are also held, and the kata is judged in much the same way figure skating and diving are judged. Participants are rated both on the degree of difficulty of their kata and on how well they execute it.

In modern judo, competition has become very important. In some respects judo has changed once again since Kano's time, and has now become more a sport than a budo art. This new emphasis is different from Kano's original *do* concept of judo, practiced mainly for character building and competition against oneself. Sport judo is primarily competition against others for rewards and trophies.

While competition is not a bad thing in itself, people today sometimes try to win at all costs, something which would have made Kano very unhappy. Sometimes judoka sacrifice good technique if they find that using brute force will get them the desired trophy. Lamenting this state of affairs, one sensei recently said, "Remember that if you win in competition after competition, the very best you can be is Grand Champion with lots of trophies, but someday this will pass. If you develop the *do* aspect of judo, however, then you've got yourself, forever."

There are, on the other hand, many valuable aspects to sport judo, and many outstanding judo competitors who always use beautiful technique. Says judo sensei Shiro Oishi:

I believe that judo is a great sport, and I have great respect for sports. It is in sports that people try, through concentrated, hard practice, to do their very best. Because your opponent does the same thing, competitors usually have great respect for each other.

The part I like the best is when you actually face your opponent on the mat. At this point it is just you alone and all that you can bring with you. No one can help you. And it's exactly the same in life. You have to learn to stand up by yourself in life.

But often in a tournament, especially in a children's tournament, parents come and cheer on their children, yelling from the sidelines, "Get him, Georgie," telling them to do this throw and that. But I don't like this. Parents should understand that the point of the competition is for the children to learn to be on their own.

On winning, Oishi says,

Of course winning is important, just as one should try to have good grades in school, but all the hard work you've done before the shiai has been done, whether you win or lose, so winning is not all there is to it. Moreover, since there may be one hundred competitors and there can only be one winner, winning just can't be everything. The important thing is putting yourself forward fully, setting high goals for yourself, and then trying time and time again, even if you keep losing.

What one gains from judo at its best—whether sport or *do* judo—really has little to do with trophies, black belts, or even judo skills themselves. Kano said that judo training was meant not only "to develop a strong and healthy body, but also to create in a man or woman perfect control over mind and body" in all spheres of life. "Judo is certainly the best thing that ever happened to me," says a woman player, "not only because it has taught me physical skills, but because it has taught me a lot about life outside, about how to live."

3 KARATE

Yang Chien, the emperor of China, wanted to live forever. Around the year A.D. 600, in the hope of finding a "fountain of youth" somewhere beyond China's borders, he sent out several sea expeditions on the search. Before long one of the expeditions happened upon a chain of rugged islands off the coast of China, where, unfortunately, the explorers did not discover any life-giving potions. Instead, they found numerous beautiful beaches and lush vegetation. Many of the ship's passengers remained on these islands, especially on the largest one, called Okinawa. With this episode began what was to be centuries of contact between the Chinese and Okinawan peoples, and many years of strong Chinese influence on Okinawan life.

The martial arts of Okinawa were also strongly influenced by China. In 1429 a man named Sho Hashi became ruler of Okinawa. To make his position stronger, he decided to take away all weapons from the Okinawan people. Soldiers were sent out to collect knives, spears, and even old rusty swords from the people of the island. Hashi placed guards outside the warehouses, where day after day mounds of unused weapons piled up.

Oddly, the same thing happened again in 1609, when the powerful Satsuma clan of Japan conquered the islands. The Satsumas ruled the Okinawans for many years, and they too proclaimed a ban on all weapons and on the practice of any fighting arts. Anyone found with a weapon was punished severely.

The proud and spirited Okinawans, anxious to be rid of their various conquerors, as well as needing to protect themselves against the pirates and brigands who infested their waters and lands, began to develop secret ways of fighting that could not be detected by their rulers. Lacking swords and spears, they began practicing how to use their hands, feet, and other parts of their bodies as weapons instead. They also began to practice ways to use farm and fishing tools as weapons, for these objects were always near at hand but didn't look like weapons to the unsuspecting conquerors.

The Okinawans searched into their past for their native fighting ways, and at the same time began to look to China, which they knew had had centuries of experience in the fighting arts. In the darkness of night they sent off the best of their village youths disguised as various kinds of travelers. The youths' mission was to sail to China and seek out kung fu masters who would teach them their art. Others brought back Chinese masters who were then hired to teach the villagers kung fu.

The Okinawans diligently and secretly practiced the Chinese methods, combined them with their own ideas about fighting, and gradually developed their own martial arts which were referred to as *Okinawa-te. Te* meant "hands," and Okinawa-te meant "Okinawa hands." Sometimes the people referred to their forbidden training simply as te. This was a fine name, for not only were hands important weapons in their style, but te was also a name that sounded harmless and could be used as a code word for underground arts.

Sometimes the Okinawans also called their combat methods *kara-te*. *Kara* was the character referring to the Tang Dynasty of China, and kara-te essentially meant "Chinese hands," reflecting the important influence of Chinese kung fu on their fighting ways.

While many Okinawan karate masters continued to follow traditional Chinese training methods, the crisis situation on the island prompted many other masters to develop their own ways. Since the islanders needed te for survival, teachers often stressed the self-defense aspects of the martial arts rather than the spiritual ones. When it was necessary for the Okinawans to become powerful quickly, then masters often speeded up the training practices.

If they wanted to develop an iron palm technique quickly, instead of working gradually from striking sand, to pebbles, to rocks, and then to iron filings, they might begin immediately with rocks and iron filings. If the Chinese practiced striking into the sides of trees or other natural objects one hundred times a day, the Okinawans would do it one thousand times. If it took the Chinese one thousand days to develop strong iron palm technique, it took the Okinawans only one hundred.

Through these and other rugged exercises the Okinawans got very quick results, and as they had hoped, they developed a phenomenal bare-handed strength that could deal successfully even with armed and armored rulers. The only drawback was that they often injured their hands during this training and didn't have time to use the special herbal medicine used by kung fu practitioners to keep their hands soft and flexible. Instead their knuckles enlarged and their hands often became excessively callused and bruised.

In the darkness of night or out alone at sea, boat people began practicing how to use their oars, nets, and hooks as weapons. Women and men farm workers alone in the forests or fields practiced fighting with their sickles, called *kama*s, and with long wooden poles called *bo*s. They even used their agricultural tool, the *nunchaku*. This harmless-looking implement had two sticks connected at one end with a cord, and looked like a big nutcracker. If the Okinawans were grinding grain, the handles of their millstone, called a *tui-fa*, could be used as a weapon. The Okinawans studied ways in which the Chinese had used these same implements in their own years of trouble, and also learned how to use the three-pronged metal Chinese weapon, the *sai*.

In time, the busy-looking woman pulling in her netloads of fish, or the peaceful-looking farmer cutting grain with his sickle, became serious forces to contend with, even against the strong military occupiers. Carrying on a guerilla war in their own land, the Okinawans used their te to strike unexpectedly and secretly, trying to overthrow their Japanese occupiers, just as the Chinese had looked to their own martial arts years before to help them get rid of their foreign Manchu rulers.

Over the years, three leading schools of te developed, centered in three different Okinawan cities—Shuri, Naha, and Tomari. The te of Shuri, called *Shuri-te*, is said to have been directly related to Shaolin kung fu.

The style from Naha was called *Naha-te*, and apparently developed from the Wutang school in China, named after the Chinese mountain where it was practiced. *Tomari-te*, from Tomari, was influenced by both Naha-te and Shuri-te.

Countless marvelous and heroic women and men martial artists developed during these years. One of the earliest stories we have is of an Okinawan man called Chatan Yara, who in the late 1600's spent twenty years in China studying the martial arts. He studied in Fukien Province, which at that time, following the burning of the Shaolin temple, was the hub of kung fu activity.

According to legend, Yara returned to Okinawa when he was thirty-two. To reacquaint himself with his homeland, he often took long walks along the beach. One night, while in calm meditation, listening to the surf and gazing at the natural beauties of the water and sand, he was startled by a sharp scream. He rushed ahead to find a husky Japanese soldier attacking a lone woman. "Stop," yelled Yara. "Why should a proud soldier like you want to attack this woman?" "Go away, boy," replied the soldier, swiftly drawing his sword. Yara suddenly realized with a shock that his days of training were over, for the soldier was intent on doing battle with him. As the angry soldier took one step forward with the sword outstretched in front of him, Yara was seized with panic. Suddenly he remembered what his teacher had said long ago: "Unless your mind is calm, you will never be able to concentrate." Now as the soldier stepped closer and closer, Yara began to regain his calm. A poor move would surely be his death.

Yara fighting Japanese soldier. Weapons (clockwise from top left): nunchaku; kama (sickle); sai; tui-fa.

As the soldier swung his sword, Yara quickly stepped back and avoided the first cut. The soldier kept advancing and Yara knew he had to stay out of range.

Meanwhile, the woman cleverly grabbed an oar from a boat nearby, quietly crept near Yara, and quickly threw it to him. With the oar, Yara now had a chance. This time as the soldier swiftly attacked, Yara expertly swung his oar, knocking the sword downward and out of the soldier's hand. At the same time, he powerfully kicked the soldier, knocking him unconscious.

To help Yara avoid the Japanese soldiers who would surely hunt him down for this act, the woman took him to her village in the mountains. Here Chatan Yara remained for many years, teaching his arts quietly to the villagers. In time he became a legendary hero to the Okinawans, and many great masters came to visit and study with him. Numerous young men, anxious to make a quick reputation against this great man (who was somewhat like "the fastest gun in the West"), also came to challenge him.

One such challenger was a famous man named Shiroma. Yara accepted his challenge and they decided to fight each other with sais. On the appointed day, Yara arose just before dawn and made his way down the mountainside to meet Shiroma on the beach. When he arrived he saw the shadowy outline of his opponent through the early morning mist. He walked toward Shiroma slowly, and the two men faced each other.

Yara, by now a veteran of many matches, showed great confidence and stood totally relaxed, his sai at his side. Shiroma, knowing then that he was up against a great master, devised a clever plan. As the sun began to rise over the horizon, Shiroma planned to maneuver so that his own back would be to the sun, while Yara would have the sun shining directly into his eyes, momentarily blinding him. With just one more step to go, Shiroma moved very slowly so that Yara would not be aware of the trap. Shiroma took the final step and moved to attack. Instantly Yara picked up his sai, reflecting the blinding sun back into Shiroma's eyes, blinding him instead. Yara then attacked Shiroma with a powerful kick, defeating him at his own game.

Later, when Shiroma came to after having been knocked unconscious, he realized the greatness of Yara, who was not only calm in the face of danger, but also displayed brilliant ingenuity in the use of his weapon.

Several years later, in the area of Shuri, two very colorful characters dominated the karate scene, the husband called Matsumura, the wife Yonamine Chiru. Matsumura's teacher, and some say even Matsumura himself, had studied Shaolin kung fu in China. Yonamine Chiru came from a very famous Okinawan karate family. Both were considered formidable Shuri-te fighters.

According to legend, one evening Yonamine and her husband dressed up in their best clothes and ventured out to visit relatives. As the evening progressed, Matsumura and several others proceeded to get a little drunk and rowdy. Yonamine, anxious to get home to attend to some business, decided to leave early on her own. On the way home, however, she was attacked by three rapists. Perfectly able to handle the situation, she used her Shuri-te to take care of the three men.

Later in the evening Matsumura staggered home with his friends. Suddenly he came upon three disheveled, black-eyed, messed-up men tied to a tree with the sash from Yonamine's dress. Understanding instantly what had happened, Matsumura smiled to himself and mused, "Ah, these men certainly picked on the wrong woman tonight."

This is just one of the many stories about this strong couple who were not only great themselves, but who also produced generations of Matsumuras who were karate masters as well. One of these later Matsumuras even taught a young man who in time became known as the "father" of Japanese karate.

Gichin Funakoshi was born in Shuri in 1868, just eight years after the birth of the founder of judo, Jigaro Kano. Like Kano, Gichin was also a small and sickly child. Following his father, who was an expert in the use of the bo, the boy began studying Shuri-te at the age of thirteen. During this period, karate was still practiced secretly, and young Funakoshi would sneak out at night, making his way by lantern to the house of his teacher, Master Azato, where he was at first the only student. In later years he also studied with Masters Itosu and Matsumura.

After studying karate for some time, Funakoshi got stronger, tougher, healthier, and increasingly serious about his training. He became so dedicated, in fact, that once during the middle of a typhoon, when other people huddled inside their homes frightened of the storm, Gichin climbed up on the slippery wet tiles of the roof of his house. Here he put himself into a Horse Stance, gritted his teeth, and tried to test the strength of his stance against the force of the gale winds and rains. His body became totally mud covered from being blown off the roof time and time again, yet he kept reappearing to try one more time.

Over the years, because of such perserverance, Funakoshi became highly skilled. During this period he also married, and his wife (whose name unfortunately is unknown) also became skilled at karate. Gichin reports that when his wife tired from her daily chores she didn't lie down to rest, but instead went outside into the yard to practice karate. Funakoshi says, "In due course she became so adept that her movements were as dextrous as those of an expert." At this time, Funakoshi had also begun teaching a few students of his own. When he wasn't home, his wife would often go outside where the students practiced and give them pointers on their karate.

In the early 1900's, with the passage of time, the secrecy surrounding karate began to wear away. The Okinawan government, realizing that all people could benefit physically and mentally from karate training, even began to have it taught in the public schools. Funakoshi by this time was a recognized master of karate and was often called upon to give exhibitions of the art around the island. At one such demonstration, in 1921, Crown Prince Hirohito of Japan, who was touring Okinawa, saw Funakoshi and was so impressed that he told everyone back home about it. Soon Funakoshi was invited to sail to Japan to demonstrate Okinawan karate for the first time to the Japanese people.

In 1923, this barely five-foot-tall, middle-aged man performed his Okinawan karate techniques in Tokyo, and proceeded to flabbergast the masters of the various Japanese arts (who were not so easy to astonish). Many of these Japanese observers wanted to test their skills against Funakoshi, and were quite surprised at how easily this tiny man defeated them, improving upon some of their own techniques with his new methods.

Seated among the notables at this demonstration was none other than Jigaro Kano. Kano was so thrilled with the exhibition that he asked Funakoshi to please teach him some of this new karate. Funakoshi agreed and went to the Kodokan a few times, where he taught Kano and his students some basic karate techniques. He also introduced some throws that are still used in judo today.

Funakoshi originally planned to return to Okinawa after his demonstration, but so many other Japanese people wanted to learn karate from him that he decided to stay. During his first years in Japan, Funakoshi was very poor. He lived in a dormitory for Okinawan students and, to pay for his room, did odd jobs as a watchman, a caretaker, gardener, and even a room sweeper. He even gave free karate lessons to the cook in exchange for better food prices. Funakoshi himself remembers the day a newspaper reporter came to the dormitory while he was sweeping the garden path:

"Where can I find Mr. Funakoshi, the karate teacher?" he inquired. "One moment, sir," I replied, and scurried away. I went quickly up to my room, changed into my formal kimono, and then descended to the entranceway where the reporter was waiting. "How do you do?" I said. "I'm Funakoshi." I shall never forget the expression of astonishment on the reporter's face when he realized that the gardener and the karate teacher were one and the same!"

Gradually, the Japanese people fell in love with karate, and by 1932 it was being taught in almost all Japanese universities. More and more students came to Funakoshi for lessons, and in 1936 he opened a big school in Tokyo, calling it *Shotokan. Shoto* was the pen name he used for writing, and *kan* meant "hall," so *Shotokan* meant "Shoto's Hall." In time, however, Funakoshi's vigorous style of Shuri-te itself began to be known as the Shotokan karate style. It is still called by this name, and has become a popular style practiced the world over.

During the 1930's, Funakoshi made a change in the word *karate* to reflect the growing "Japanization" of the Okinawan art. He altered the writing of the characters which meant "Chinese hand" to mean "empty hand." Both writings, however, are pronounced the same. It is Funakoshi's writing of *karate* that is used throughout the world today. Moreover, just as Kano had once changed the word *jujutsu* to *judo*, so too Funakoshi now began calling karate *karate-do*, meaning "the way of the empty hand." This mirrored the change in karate practice from a rugged guerilla-warfare art to one practiced in both Okinawa and Japan primarily for physical health, character building, and spiritual development. Funakoshi said many times, "The ultimate aim of the art of karate lies not in victory or defeat, but in the perfection of the character of its participants."

As Gichin Funakoshi got older and older, he still remained strong and highly skilled. A story is told that when he was in his sixties one of his students, Masatomo Takagi, caught him napping and decided to sneak up on him. Just as the student attacked, Funakoshi jumped up, successfully blocking the attack even as he was getting up. Takagi also says that in daily training he could never break through Funakoshi's defense, even though he tried repeatedly.

Funakoshi, who also loved to spend his free time doing calligraphy and writing poetry, lived to be very old. He said that despite his sickly childhood, he lived to a healthy old age because of his lifelong study of karate.

Other famous Okinawan masters of different te styles followed Funakoshi to Japan. In the late 1920's, Chojun Miyagi brought a style of Naha-te to Japan which was called *goju*. According to legend, this style acquired its name in the following way: One day karate practitioners from the Okinawan city of Naha attended a martial-arts conference where, to their surprise, they were asked to identify their style by name. Since they had never had to give their te a specific name before, other than Naha-te, they described it to the people. "Well," they said, "it's a little bit hard, like this, and a little soft, like this."

Master Miyagi, quite enchanted by this explanation, thereafter began to call his te style goju—*go* meaning "hard" and *ju* meaning "soft."

Miyagi was followed in 1930 by Okinawan Master Kenwa Mabuni, who had studied te from both Shuri and Naha. He introduced to Japan a style called *shito*, a word made from a combination of the names of his two teachers.

Just as the Okinawans had developed their own distinct styles from Chinese kung fu, so too the Japanese now began to develop their own styles from the Okinawan systems. In addition to Shotokan, goju, and shito, there were many other fascinating masters and wonderful styles of Japanese karate. All of the styles—and there are as many as seventy today—have their merits, and there is really no such thing as "the best style." Much depends upon the skill of the individual practitioners.

Karate next traveled from Japan to Korea. The Koreans already had been strongly influenced by the Chinese martial arts, and had practiced the various kung fu styles for centuries. From 1909 to 1945, however, Japan took control of Korea, just as they had earlier taken over Okinawa. They also banned the practice of the Korean martial arts. As a result, over this thirty-five-year period many of the Chinese arts that had been practiced in Korea were lost. In their place the Japanese introduced many of their own martial arts, especially *kendo*, judo, and karate. Some Koreans also went to Japan to study, and quite a few even trained with Master Funakoshi himself.

Gradually the Koreans took from the Japanese and developed their own brand of karate. Master Won Kooh Lee opened the first *dojang* (training hall) in Seoul with a style called *chung do kwon*. These were followed by Ki Hwong's *moo duck kwon*, Song Sup Chun's *yun moo kwon*, and Pyang In Yun's *chang moo kwon*.

In 1955, General Choi of South Korea named the art *tae kwon do*. *Tae* means "smash with the feet," *kwon* means "punch," and *do*, just as in Japanese, means "the way." This term, *tae kwon do*, meaning "the way of kicking and punching," has become the generic term for all these Korean styles, parallel to the word *karate* for the Japanese and Okinawan arts. Choi is sometimes called the "father of modern tae kwon do."

In 1966, General Choi, in an effort to make tae kwon do more Korean and less Japanese, developed an entirely new system of Korean "forms" (like kung fu sets) called International Tae Kwon Do Forms. He tried, though quite unsuccessfully, to get all the individual Korean styles to adopt this one, unified national system. In 1973, Korea established the World Tae Kwon Do Federation in a further attempt to unify the art.

The major difference between the Okinawan and Japanese karate and Korean tae kwon do is that the former generally places equal emphasis on the use of both hand and leg techniques, while the Koreans tend to place about seventy percent of the emphasis upon leg techniques.

During World War II and the Korean War, many Westerners stationed in Asia were exposed to the fighting arts for the first time. Many of them studied karate in Okinawa, Japan, and tae kwon do in Korea, and brought the arts back to their home countries. In time, teachers from Japan, Okinawa, and Korea also came to the West to help teach. Karate is now popular the world over, and some say there are several million practitioners.

Karate became especially popular in the United States. People study it for character building, good health, self-defense, and sport competition. Moreover, carrying on karate's traditions of the past, many of the liberation movements of the 1960's and 1970's—movements of the Third World peoples as well as the women's movement—have looked to karate once again as a means of giving people strength of body as well as dignity and pride in their struggles.

KARATE MYTHS: WHAT KARATE IS AND ISN'T

Today when we conjure up an image of karate, we picture a man gritting his teeth as he smashes through a pile of boards with a "karate chop." His hands, of course, have huge knuckles and calluses all over. Or we imagine him doing a flashy side kick while flying through the air six feet above the ground. Much to our surprise, these images, gleaned perhaps from legends of karate's Okinawan past, or made popular by today's movies and comics, are distorted views of what karate today is all about.

98

A modern-day karate student once asked his teacher, "Sensei, tell me please, how many boards can you break?" "Why, I can't break any," replied the sensei with a slight smile. "But sensei," answered the surprised student, "how can you be a karate teacher if you can't even break boards?" "You tell me," said the sensei, "how many boards have attacked you lately?"

The teacher's message is simple. Boards do not hit people. Why, then, are people so intent upon hitting boards? Indeed, *karateka* (a Japanese word for "karate practitioners") can and do break boards and bricks. Yet they do so primarily for demonstration purposes. Breaking boards in itself is almost never used as a karate training device on a day-to-day basis.

The karate-chop hand position, or more correctly, a "knife hand," is really only one of many karate weapons. The more widely used weapon is the fist. It is the fist, not the "chop" (a word never used in karate), that is usually used as the symbol of karate by karateka themselves.

A proper fist is made in this way: First clench the fingers of your hand tightly together into a ball. Squeeze as firmly as you can, as if trying to get all the air out of your fist. Then close your thumb tightly over your first two fingers, binding your fingers together firmly.

This fist is used in several karate techniques, and most often in the straight punch. Here it is used in a "forefist" position, and the first two knuckles of the hand are the part of the hand that strikes the target first. The fist is also used for the "back-fist strike," in which you hit with the same knuckles but use the back of the fist rather than the front. The "hammer-fist strike" uses the same fist again, yet here one strikes like a hammer with the side of one's fist rather than with the knuckles.

Sometimes karateka attack with open-fingered hand techniques such as the "spear-hand thrust," the "palm-heel strike," the "ridge-hand strike," and the famous "knife-hand strike"—each using different parts of the hand as a weapon. As in kung fu, some hand positions have animal names, such as "Tiger-mouth hand," "Chicken-head wrist," and "Ox-jaw hand."

The reknowned karate "knuckles"—those extra-large, knotty protuberances on the karateka's hands—these too, like the "chop," are not all that common. Long removed from their early Okinawan origins, few karate schools today encourage the building of such knuckles. To do so involves damaging the hands, and large knuckles are not necessary for good karate technique.

To find out if a person is a karateka, sneak a look at their feet instead of their hands. While an experienced karateka's hands may be smooth, it would be unlikely to find one who did not have large calluses on the balls and heels of the feet, built up unavoidably from years and years of moving from stance to stance in bare feet.

While there is indeed much kicking in karate, it is also wrong to associate karate with the flying side kick— a technique used even less often than the karate "chop." To the karate player, the front kick, side kick, and roundhouse kick, all executed from the floor, are more basic. Flying kicks, performed while in the air, are spectacular to watch but difficult to do. And if a player

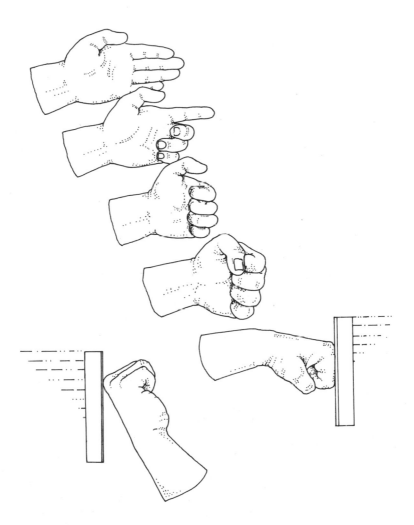

Fist making; straight punch; back fist.

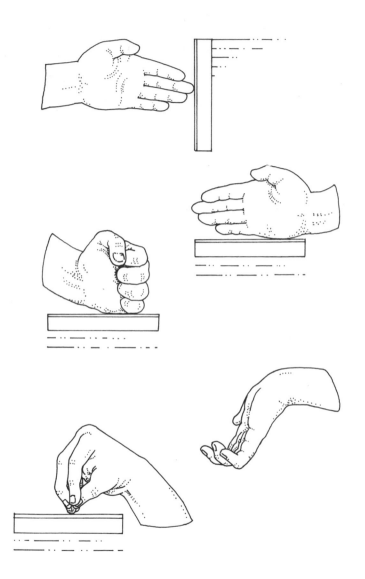

Top to bottom: spear hand; knife hand; hammer fist; palm heel; chicken-head wrist.

misses the target, he or she is in a helpless position in the air while the opponent is in a balanced position on the ground. Being rooted is an important concept in karate, and flying kicks are used only in very special circumstances.

Finally, the idea that the karate practitioner is always male is incorrect. Karate is designed so that anyone, of any size, shape, age, or sex, can do the art successfully. Power does not depend on body structure, but comes from using correct karate principles. While in the past the activity was certainly dominated by men, recently— during the 1960's and 1970's—more and more women all over the world have become karateka and many of them excellent. When you read the word *karateka*, you should picture both women and men, as well as girls and boys.

One might ask, If the legendary karate power does not come from huge knuckles, or from the famous "chop," where does it come from? The secret of karate power, as of other martial arts, lies in following certain principles of proper technique—using one's entire body, mind, and spirit in just the right way.

A description of how to execute a karate punch will help explain some of these karate principles. Picture a karateka standing in a straight and natural posture. The only part of the body that has any tension is a special part called the *tant'ien* (a Chinese word.) The tant'ien is that point on the body about two inches below the belly button. In Eastern thought, this point is considered to be the center of balance and strength in the human body.

Karate punch series.

The karateka's hands are held in fists at his or her sides, just above the hips, palms facing upward. The arms and shoulders are relaxed (not limp, but relaxed). The person starts moving one hand out toward the target in front of him, the elbow rubbing close against the body as the arm moves forward. The arm thrusts straight forward and at the last moment, before the arm is completely extended, the fist twists like a corkscrew so that the palm faces downward as it strikes the target. The body is relaxed until the point of contact, and at this moment the tant'ien tightens completely and creates a chain reaction, with all the muscles of the body tightening as a unit. This happens for only a fraction of a second while the punch is executed, and then the body relaxes again, preparing for the next move. The action

104

is like that of a bullwhip used in a circus, where the whip goes out relaxed and fluid, but at the end becomes rigid and cracks.

The concentration of all one's energy on one specific target for one instant is called *focusing*. This principle of focus is used in all karate punching, striking, blocking, and kicking. If there is one "secret" to karate, it is in this dynamic of relaxing and tensing. It is this special coordination of mind and body that makes a karate punch different from and more powerful than an ordinary street-fighting punch.

The karateka with a well-focused technique will also *kiai*, or let out a loud shout. This yelling helps the karateka focus their energies. More than this, the yell itself can have a powerful effect against opponents. It is said that some masters could give forth shouts that would stop their adversaries dead in their tracks.

But *kiai* means more than yelling, for it is, in essence, a ch'i technique. The word itself means "the coming together of ch'i." (The *ki* of *kiai* is the Japanese word for ch'i.) To kiai is to focus all one's ch'i in one technique, and in this sense one does not have to yell, or make any sound at all. There can be a silent kiai. Some masters, including Funakoshi's teacher, Master Matsumura, were able to develop "kiai of the eyes," whereby all their ch'i could be expelled from their eyes, repelling the attacker like a bolt of lightning. Perhaps the expression "if looks could kill" came from just such a master. The silent kiai of some masters could actually produce a kind of invisible-force field around their bodies that acted as a shield against attack. Opponents found that when they faced the master in a match, they somehow just couldn't begin to attack. On eye contact they would feel weak and inept, and would know they had been defeated.

While such high development of the kiai is very advanced and beyond the abilities of the average student, development of such control is the ultimate aim of all martial artists.

TRAINING

One enters a Japanese or Okinawan dojo or Korean dojang (training hall) in much the same manner—with a serious and respectful feeling. Shoes are taken off and never worn in the workout area. The interiors of most karate schools are the same, usually very simple with a bare floor. When they enter, students change into their karate uniforms—pajamalike tops, and loose pants tied with a drawstring. Karate uniforms, also called gis, look very much like judo gis, but they are of lighter weight since karate doesn't involve very much pulling and tugging on a partner's uniform. As in judo, uniforms are held together by belts of different colors signifying the rank of the students.

Rank

Many different martial-arts systems make use of the black belt as a symbol of high rank or skill. But where did the idea for the black belt come from? One story tells us that it originated in China. According to this legend, when the Chinese people first began to study their various fighting arts, they trained in the grassy fields near their homes. Students sometimes wore white outfits tied with white sashes or belts. From the many falls and rolls they took on the ground, their uniforms became green with grass stains. People washed their uniforms often, but not their belts, which became greener and greener. When the grass wore out from the constant onslaught of many moving feet, the students were left to work out in the dirt. Again, uniforms got dirty and were washed, but the belts became darker and darker brown in color. Eventually, when students had trained a very long time, their belts became black with wear—a sure sign that they had been studying kung fu for some years.

Over the years people have given all kinds of meanings to various belts, but the black belt has remained a symbol of attainment of skill. A first-degree black belt is a mark not of an "expert," but of an experienced student as opposed to a beginner. It takes an average of three to four years to attain this rank.

In most karate systems, as in judo, there are dan rankings, meaning "grade" or "degree," and kyu rankings—called *kup* in Korean—meaning "class." Karate students can climb from the first dan or first-degree black belt up to the tenth degree (although only one or two top masters have ever attained tenth degree). Before students achieve any dan rankings there are usually eight kyu rankings they must pass, number one being the highest. In some ways, kyu ranks are like elementary school, first dan is like high school, and the higher dans are like college. Also as in school, the exams for each rank become harder and harder the higher up you go.

Unlike judo, karate systems are not at all uniform, and each system has slightly different ranking systems and color symbols. A goju tenth dan might wear a red belt, a Shotokan master a black one. In kyu ranks, one often sees the influence of the Chinese legend, with students usually being advancing from white belt, to green, and then to brown, before finally attaining the black belt. Other systems use blue, orange, and purple belts. Moreover, the qualifications for promotion to different kyus and dans differ with each style.

Basic Training

While the actions of the students, the physical layout of the dojo, and the exact procedure may differ from place to place, a typical class in any karate school today might be like the following:

Before stepping out onto the training floor, students bow as a sign of respect for the area. At the start of class students line up according to rank. Then, on command, they do a few moments of meditation. This is done to clear their minds of outside worries and thoughts so they can concentrate completely on the class. Then the instructor and students bow to each other. The class begins.

The instructor or senior student leads warm-up exercises—stretching, push-ups, and sit-ups—in preparation for a workout in basics. Students then line up on the floor for basic practice. Basics are those stances, kicks, punches, strikes, and blocks that are fundamental to each individual style. While all styles are different, each has four or five basic stances, blocks, strikes, punches, and kicks that form the core of its style—the alphabet upon which all else is built.

In a typical class students might start out doing moving punches, called *lunge punches.* Someone will count, "one, two, three, turn, one, two, three, turn," and on each count the students will move and punch, up and down the floor. They might do fifty lunge punches in this way, followed by fifty moving face blocks done in front stance, fifty stomach blocks in the same stance, fifty knife-hand blocks in back stance, fifty front kicks, and fifty roundhouse kicks.

Forms

Suddenly, the pace of the class changes. On a command, students quickly assume new positions on the floor, and while the teacher counts, the students move in unison through a beautiful pattern of varied movements. The students move perfectly together, as if they were performing a well-rehearsed, synchronized dance routine.

The students are doing "forms"—called *kata*s in Japanese and Okinawan, *hyung*s in Korean. Karate forms, like the katas of judo and the sets of kung fu, are the formal exercises of karate. Forms are the essence of karate. They are the heart, the root of all the basic moves and principles of any karate system. Most of the forms practiced today—and there may be as many as fifty in any one karate style—were created centuries ago by Chinese masters and have been passed on to us with the modifications made in the course of their travels through time.

As in kung fu, forms are organized sets of techniques performed in special sequence alone against imaginary opponents, and sometimes practiced with partners who also do prearranged movements. Students sometimes practice together, or they might work out alone, practicing their own individual speed and timing. In one class they might drill one form eight times, or perhaps eight different forms one time each.

Many people think karate consists mostly of free-fighting with partners, and unless they have visited a karate school or seen a karate tournament, it is unlikely they will ever have seen or heard of "forms." Yet there was once a time, before there was any free-sparring, when form training was the primary way in which karate was taught. When Funakoshi was a young boy, this was true. He recalls:

Night after night . . . in the backyard of the Azato house as the master looked on, I would practice a kata . . . time and again week after week, sometimes month after month, until I had mastered it to my teacher's satisfaction. This constant repetition of a single kata was grueling, often exasperating, and on occasion humiliating. . . . But practice was strict, and I was never permitted to move on to another kata until Azato was convinced that I had satisfactorily understood the one I had been working on.

Many traditional schools still practice this way, using forms as the primary teaching device of the system.

All forms, regardless of the style, consist of the various hand, foot, shifting, and blocking techniques of the style, practiced in all directions and in many combinations. They range from simple to extremely complicated. Some require great agility—almost acrobatic skills—to perform. Others are designed to develop muscular and breathing coordination. Some forms have only fifteen moves and others as many as one hundred. They may take from thirty seconds to two minutes to perform. Almost all forms begin and end at the same spot. While one may kick and leap and punch all over the floor during the performance of the form, after the last move one should be standing on the exact spot where one started.

All the forms are very difficult to perfect, and while a twenty-move kata might take only thirty seconds to perform, it might take twenty years to learn how to perform those thirty seconds correctly.

Form practice is especially difficult for the karateka because one competes with oneself. You are your own opponent. If you walk off, you are only walking out on yourself. From the first move to the last, there is nobody around but you and your kata.

It is because of this difficulty—because it is hardest of all to compete against oneself—that form training has always been so important to karate. It is through form practice that one builds that fighting spirit without which one cannot succeed in karate.

Free-fighting

The pace once again changes dramatically, and the students hurry to take partners. They bow to each other respectfully and then, on command, begin free-fighting, also called free-sparring. They do this exercise, changing partners every few minutes to experience fighting with all sizes and skill levels in the class.

Free-fighting is often the most exciting part of karate for both the players and the spectators. It is also the most frightening for the fighters, because they face real partners who can attack them at any time with any and all techniques. Anything goes at any time. Hence the name *free*-sparring. Free-sparring has much the same place in karate that randori has in judo.

In free-sparring, the students apply all they have learned in basics and form to the new situation. Without a good background in both, this exercise will be very hard. Attacks come quickly. There is little time to think. The player must react immediately with reflex action. Sparring is certainly not the time, for example, to learn how to block a kick. In much the same way, baseball players don't wait until an actual game to learn how to catch or throw or pitch. They must practice these fundamentals separately, every day at the park, so that in a game, when they have to move and think fast, they can do so automatically without making a lot of mistakes.

The idea of free-fighting in karate is quite new. In the past, when karate practitioners had serious matches with each other they did so to challenge each other's fighting skills, or because they were angry. People were killed or seriously injured in such fights. Gradually things changed, and karate became a slightly milder activity. The idea of focusing a blow just short of actually hitting one's opponent came into being. Karateka learned to control their "perfect" techniques so they could land a full-powered move, but do so just a fraction of an inch from their target. It was not until this idea became popular that Funakoshi, in 1936, initiated free-sparring as regular training practice.

It was at this time that the seeds of sport karate were planted. The idea of people competing for prizes and trophies in free-sparring, and kata as well, gradually

Free sparring in karate.

took hold. Sport karate became increasingly popular and widespread starting in the 1940's. While competition was originally limited primarily to men, in recent years, with the growing interest of women in the martial arts, tournaments now have many women in both sparring and kata. There are now some mixed kata competitions, and occasionally mixed sparring between men and women.

Many people ask, "If people just go at each other in karate matches, punching and kicking whenever and wherever they want, then how is karate really different from street fighting?"

One of the key ideas behind karate is the "one-point kill," or "one-point technique." Karateka seek perfection of their form in order to deliver the one perfect kick or punch that theoretically would completely do in the opponent.

The situation is quite different in street fighting. A street fighter is not concerned about self-development, and doesn't care at all about perfect form. This is why her techniques are ineffective and she would lose to a trained karateka.

If you watched two street fighters in a match, you would probably see a lot of action. The two opponents would fight wildly, flailing about like two monkeys wrestling in a cage. But to watch karate masters in a fight would be entirely different. They would resemble, instead, tigers stalking their prey. There would be no wasted action. They would concentrate for a long time, looking for a weakness in the opponent's defense that would give them the chance for that one perfect technique. The weak spot is not always physical, but sometimes spiritual as well. The karateka looks not only to see whether the opponent is off balance, but also to see if she or he is mentally off guard. With true karate masters, one would see almost no physical movement between the two, but one would feel strong vibrations, tensions, a definite aura of power in the air. While both may stare, immobile, into each other's eyes, there is tremendous action on the mental plain, with both masters dueling with each other on this invisible level.

One might ask, "Can a karateka beat a judoka?" The question is silly and can't be answered. It's like asking who is a better athlete, a basketball player or a swimmer. They are two different things. A basketball player might not know how to swim, and the swimmer might not know how to shoot a basket, but it doesn't mean that either is a better or worse athlete. To compare a judoka and a karateka is to do the same thing. Neither is a better fighter. They are just different from each other.

Supplementary Training

The *thump thump* that one might hear on first entering a karate school is the sound of a person hitting a *makiwara*. This is a punching board that looks something like a parking meter, only it is made of wood and is very flexible. The striking area of the board is made of either straw rope or some kind of padding like sponge rubber, topped with a canvaslike cover to prevent damage to the knuckles.

Students practice at the makiwara by getting into a

stance their style favors, and then striking the makiwara repeatedly with various hand techniques. At one session a karateka might do fifty straight punches, followed by fifty back-fist strikes with the right hand, and then with the left. Students practice this way to give them a feeling of what it's like to contact a real target, since they mostly practice by punching into the air. It also helps them develop stronger wrists, arms, and hands.

Another type of training for punching (although it is quite exotic and would not be done regularly in most schools) is *candle practice*. You light a candle and place the flame about a half inch to an inch away from your fist, which is extended in a punch position. You then withdraw your hand and practice punching at the flame, trying to extinguish it with air fanned by the speed of your hand. It would be cheating to punch your fist into the flame, and might also burn your hand. At advanced levels, you move your fist back from one to two inches, and then three inches away from the flame, making it increasingly difficult. While it is fun to practice, this exercise is definitely supplementary to basic karate training.

One interesting training device for developing strong karate legs and feet is the *iron geta*. Getas are iron sandals fashioned after the traditional Japanese wooden sandal. They weigh from three to ten pounds, and the practitioners put them on and kick in special ways. Legs, ankles, and even toes are strengthened by this practice, and kicks become much quicker. This exercise should always be done with an instructor, for done improperly, it will only make your kicks slower and less powerful.

There are sometimes other training devices in a dojo, such as heavy bags hanging from the ceiling, buckets of sand, weights for punching work, speed bags, and even mats for practicing throwing techniques.

Never Say Can't

Karate training is difficult for everybody, and not only because one is expected to do hundreds of kicks and punches in any regular class. There is more.

It is, for sure, on the very coldest day of the year, when there is frost on the ground and a good strong wind, that the instructor takes the students outside to train. The sweat freezes on your eyelashes, your gi is so cold it feels like cardboard, and your toes are completely numb as you front kick.

For those who don't mind the cold there is always summer training. On a hundred-degree day in August, when people are too hot even to walk down the street, the karate students are taken for a run outside, farther than they have ever run in their lives, and then brought back to the dojo to work out some more—with the windows closed.

To the outsider this looks like madness, but important lessons are being taught. Much to their surprise the students survive, and learn that not only did they *not* get terrible colds or frostbite in winter, or pass out and melt into puddles in summer, but they even felt good after the workouts.

The same lessons are being taught day after day in regular karate training. Classes are usually very difficult. To outsiders the senseis, who often stalk the room barking commands in sharp tones, must seem very mean. They push students until the students are sure they can't lift their legs for one more kick. Just at this point, teachers make them do twenty more. Funakoshi remembers that when he trained with Azato, the master "would murmur 'Do it again' or 'A little more!' A little more, a little more, so often a little more, until the sweat poured and I was ready to drop."

Students learn they are expected never to quit in the middle of a class just because they think it's too hard. There is no quitting in karate. There is no "I can't."

What people learn from this is not that their teacher is cruel, but rather that their own bodies and minds can do much more than they ever dreamed possible. They learn that most of the limits they put on themselves were just made up in their own heads, and are not real at all. They learn that their sensei is a kind person for having taught them this.

Karateka slowly begin to push themselves on their own, even when the teacher isn't looking. This is as it should be, for the goal of karate is to seek one's own perfection, not just the teacher's approval. Since perfection is the goal, and few are perfect, compliments from teachers are rare. It is understood that students should try to do each punch and each kick as well as they possibly can, with good stance and good focus every time, even if they do them one hundred times each. This is very hard to do, but if karateka try hard on each technique, it becomes easier rather than more difficult. The more they concentrate on doing things just right, the more they forget the pain and the sweat. Before they know it the workout is over. On the other hand, if they think, "Oh, no, I'll never make it through" or "I wonder if I can cheat a little bit when the sensei isn't looking," then the whole class is harder because they're thinking about the pain.

All of these disciplines are designed to strengthen a karateka's will or spirit. Without spirit, karate will not work. In some ways spirit is like electric current, for while one might have a beautiful TV set, if there is no current, it will not work. In the same way, one might have a beautiful, strong body, capable of doing marvelous karate techniques, but without the proper will or spirit, nothing will happen, and one will still be a poor karateka.

Being on the karate floor is much the same as being in life. The lessons learned about karate are lessons learned about living. When you learn not to quit on the dojo floor, and decide to take on the fight, you are also learning not to quit on yourself in life.

Often, if you are playing a game with a friend and you find you are losing, you want to quit, and you say things like "I don't like this game. I didn't want to play anyway." The winner usually says, "No, this is a great game. Let's play one more time." The better way is to try your very hardest no matter what—to enjoy the trying and not give up. Then, even if you lose, you know at least that you did not quit on yourself. While you might be angry that you lost, you are not angry with yourself. Life is much better played this way.

4 AIKIDO and T'AI CHI CH'UAN

Thousands of years ago in China, from about 640 B.C. to 479 B.C., there lived a man named Lao-tze, or "Old Sage." He was called a sage because he was such a wise man, and legend has it that when he was born he already had the wisdom of an eighty-year-old person. Because of this notion, many paintings of Lao-tze depict him with a long gray beard even as a baby.

In his famous book, the *Tao Te Ching*, Lao-tze said the most important thing in life is for people to be in harmony with nature and in balance with the universe. To gain this harmony and balance, it is necessary to follow a certain path, or "way," called *Tao* in Chinese. Over the centuries many people read, thought about, and followed Lao-tze's ideas about Tao. Along with other important philosophies such as Confucianism and Buddhism, Lao-tze's ideas, called *Taoism*, greatly influenced all areas of Asian culture, including the martial arts. In fact the idea of *do* in the Japanese martial arts came directly from Lao-tze's idea of Tao, and both words are written with the same character.

Two martial arts particularly affected by Taoist thought are t'ai chi ch'uan of China and aikido of Japan. Both arts, for example, follow very seriously the Taoist idea of "softness." Said Lao-tze, "When people are alive, they are soft and supple. When they are dead, they become hard and rigid. When a plant is living, it is soft and tender. When it is dead, it becomes withered

Lao-tze riding on a sacred cow.

and dry. Hence, the hard and rigid belongs to the company of the dead. The soft and supple belongs to the company of the living. . . . The softest of all things overrides the hardest of all things." A hard stone, for example, can be worn away by soft, dripping water.

But how can one attain such a quality? Lao-tze felt that if people could develop their ch'i, their "inner life force," they could then attain the softness (the "pliability," he called it) of a baby. In line with this thinking, both t'ai chi ch'uan and aikido place tremendous importance on developing ch'i (ki in Japanese). "Pour out your ki, lead your opponent's ki," says the aikido sensei to the students. "Relax and let your ch'i flow," instructs the Chinese t'ai chi sifu.

Following the laws of nature, it is wiser to bend in a storm, like a willow tree, than to stand rigid like an oak, and perhaps break in two. "Bend and you will be whole," said Lao-tze. Both aikido and t'ai chi use the idea of bending, or "yielding," as a main principle of defense. Rather than fighting an opponent by pitting one's strength against theirs, it is much smarter to yield first and then use the other person's momentum against them. If done correctly, then "four ounces can topple a thousand pounds" says a t'ai chi maxim. Said the aikido way, you can try to turn back a stream of water, but it is much easier to lead it where you wish it to go.

These two arts also follow the Taoist idea of "doing nothing to accomplish everything." Once a student asked an aikido master how to defend against a strong punching or kicking attack. The reply was, "No matter how strong an attack is, if it falls on empty space, it is useless." In others words, the best defense is to not be there when the attack comes. In t'ai chi it is the same. One master advised that if someone "tries to use force to control or push you, it is like catching the wind or shadows. Everywhere is empty. . . ."

Another story which illustrates the same idea, as well as the Taoist principle of conquering violence without using violence, is the following: Chan Doung Yi, a modern-day t'ai chi master, tells of the day many years ago when a burly gangster swaggered into his small furniture store asking for money. The teacher tried to calm him down, yet when the gangster kept up his demands, Chan finally said, "All right, you want to fight, do you? Well, let's step outside." Once on the street, the t'ai chi master casually hit a big metal lamppost causing it to shake back and forth with a loud *twang*. "If your body is as strong as this lamppost, I'll fight you," he said to the gangster. With eyes wide, the gangster ran off down the street. A few days later he returned to apologize and ask the shopkeeper to lunch. "We became good friends after that," explains Chan.

While many martial arts teach attacking as well as defending techniques, both aikido and t'ai chi rely primarily—aikido almost completely—on defensive techniques. This means that aikido players will act only when attacked first. Otherwise they will merely wait peacefully. It is impossible, in theory, for two aikido players to attack each other. T'ai chi, while mostly defensive, is slightly different. When attacked, one yields, but if the opponent retreats, one follows.

Finally, it is not surprising that both aikido and t'ai chi are concerned primarily with *not* hurting one's opponent. "The way to heaven is to benefit, not to harm," said Lao-tze. Because aikido teaches people how to defend themselves perfectly without hurting the attacker, it is sometimes called "the nonfighting martial art."

Both arts, as practiced today, are primarily *do* arts, rather than more warlike, practical jutsu arts. Moreover, neither aikido nor t'ai chi is concerned with sport competition. Practitioners want most of all to conquer themselves, not their enemies. The quest of t'ai chi ch'uan and aikido is to gain good health, a long life, and a wonderful feeling of harmony with the universe.

THE HISTORY OF T'AI CHI CH'UAN

It is very hard to find out how t'ai chi ch'uan began. The history books give us many different stories. One popular legend says the founder of t'ai chi was a Chinese Confucian and Taoist scholar by the name of Chang San Feng. He lived, some say, during the Tang Dynasty of China. According to others, he was born during the Sung Dynasty, or perhaps the Yuan, or even the Ming. In other words, he may have lived as far back as A.D. 618 or as recently as the fifteenth century.

In any event, as tradition has it, Chang San Feng was a student in the Shaolin monastery. After ten years of hard kung fu training, he had become very skilled at all the animal fighting styles, such as the Dragon, Tiger, Leopard, Snake, and Stork. Nature, however, always has more to teach, and one day while Chang was out taking a walk, he happened upon a fight between a bird and a snake. He watched as the bird dove down from the sky time after time, trying to kill a snake that had been peacefully sunning itself on a rock below. Each time the sharp-beaked bird attacked, the alert snake was able by moving its head in quick, circling movements to avoid being struck. The snake then pretended weakness, hoping to fool the bird. When the bird fell for the trick and moved in closer for a better look, the clever snake sprang and grasped the shocked bird in its fangs.

In the days that followed, Chang carefully studied the clever movements of the snake and combined his new thoughts with the fighting ways that he already knew. He also added some ideas from his Taoist philosophy, deciding that it was most important to emphasize using one's ch'i instead of relying on just muscular power. In truth, as we shall see, developing this internal energy did make people strong in entirely new and quite extraordinary ways. Because of this, Chang's new kung fu was very different from and, he thought, superior to the older Shaolin arts. It was fitting that he call his new art t'ai chi ch'uan, for the words mean "The Supreme Ultimate Fist."

Another person also credited with founding t'ai chi ch'uan was Chen Wang-ting. He is more than a legendary figure, for we know that he actually lived in China during the 1600's. As a general for the Ming Dynasty, he was highly skilled in many fighting arts, and when he finished his military service he set to work thinking of ways to make the fighting arts even more effective. Chen combined the best of all the arts he knew, and developed the one to top them all. When he found what he was looking for he, too, called his new art t'ai chi ch'uan.

This Chen style of t'ai chi, named after its founder, was passed down through the Chen family, taught carefully to the young sons and daughters for fourteen generations. No one other than a Chen was ever taught these skills until a young man arrived named Yang Lu-ch'an (1800–1872). Apparently the current Chen family t'ai chi master, Chen Ch'ang-hsing, was so impressed by Yang's wonderful martial-arts ability that he taught Yang all the secrets of the Chen family's t'ai chi.

After Yang had studied with Chen for many years, he moved from Chen's village in Honan Province to Peking, where he began to teach. His powers were said to be so great that once a young challenger punched Yang's stomach, and when Yang laughed the breath from his laugh alone sent the young man flying thirty feet across the floor. Another story tells of Yang's famous visit to the emperor of China. Supposedly, when Yang first set foot inside the beautiful palace courtyard, two ugly, sharp-toothed guard dogs surprise-attacked him, chomping at his legs. Then, strangely, these fierce dogs stopped their attack and ran off with their tails between their legs. Yang, unperturbed, proceeded into the palace with a slight smile on his lips. Later that night the emperor's dog keepers found some broken dog teeth in the palace courtyard. Yang's ch'i power had made his legs just that strong.

It is no surprise that with such a reputation this great martial artist was nicknamed "Yang the Unsurpassed," and that his own particular style of t'ai chi soon became known as the Yang style.

Yang Lu-ch'an had three sons to whom he taught his knowledge. The first son died when he was very young, but the second son, Yang Pan-hou, and the third, Yang Chien-hou (1843–1917) became highly skilled. It is said that Yang Chien-hou had developed a wonderful understanding of t'ai chi yielding. He had an acute sensitivity to the movement of others. Chien-hou could let a small bird stand on the palm of his hand, and when the bird tried to fly away by pushing off with its feet, he was able to feel the bird's energy and yield to the push. The bird then had no base to push off from and could not fly away. This might sound simple, but it is extraordinarily hard to do.

In the next generation, Yang Chien-hou's son Yang Ch'eng-fu (1883–1935) carried on the tradition. A student of his wrote in his memoirs:

One rainy day . . . my teacher . . . and I were crossing the Outer Paitu Bridge in Shanghai. A large sturdy man walking very quickly ran smack into Yang and promptly recoiled several feet onto his back. He arose and stared angrily at the quiet Yang but, apparently so surprised that he had failed to move him, walked away without speaking.

This most powerful and effective Yang style of kung fu eventually spread outside the Yang family and in time became very popular throughout China. Other t'ai chi ch'uan masters branched off from this Yang line and formed their own distinct styles. Wu Ch'ien Ch'uan (1870–1942), a student of Yang Pan-hou, started his own Wu style. A Mr. Sun and a Mr. Tung formed their own styles, the Sun and the Tung, which also became very well known.

As more and more Chinese people came to live in the United States, so too t'ai chi masters began to teach here. One such master was Cheng Man Ch'ing, mentioned in the chapter on kung fu for his versatility and excellence in many arts. Cheng, who taught t'ai chi ch'uan in New York City until his death in 1975, was not only a master of t'ai chi, but also of *go* (Chinese chess), calligraphy (Chinese penmanship), poetry, and painting. He was also a doctor of traditional Chinese medicine.

Cheng, who was born in 1901 in China's Chekiang Province, started practicing calligraphy when he was only five years old. Soon after, he began studying medicine with his mother, who was a doctor of traditional Chinese medicine. As the story goes, when Cheng was ten years old, he was badly hurt while playing with his friends in an old temple. His mother nursed and healed him, and Cheng was so impressed with her skill that he studied with her for a long time. Later, he too became such a good doctor that he was nicknamed "Cheng of one evening," referring to how quickly he could cure people's illnesses.

When he was older he lived in Peking, where he studied t'ai chi ch'uan with none other than Yang Ch'eng-fu, the powerful man on the bridge. Cheng had earlier contracted a bad case of tuberculosis, and credited t'ai chi with having cured him, giving him "fifty years of extra life," as he put it. Although Cheng trained very hard, it was not until he cured Yang's wife of a serious illness that Yang taught him all his secrets to show his gratitude. Cheng later moved to New York City, where for many years he taught his wisdom.

Because of masters like Cheng Man Ch'ing, t'ai chi has become popular the world over. It is not uncommon to find t'ai chi practitioners, the young and the old, joyously practicing their t'ai chi early in the morning in the countryside and city parks in many countries of the world. While t'ai chi was once used for self-defense, people now practice it mainly as an "art of life," a way to gain a healthy body and a peaceful mind. Moreover, many believe that learning t'ai chi will guarantee them a longer lifetime. Yang Chien, a Chinese emperor of the seventh century who sent ships abroad to find the "fountain of youth," would have done better to look within his own country, for it was in t'ai chi that this answer lay.

Despite this emphasis on long life and health, t'ai chi is, nonetheless, a complete system of kung fu and can be practiced as such. While teaching methods vary from school to school, a t'ai chi training session might be something like the following:

T'ai Chi Training

Students wearing dungarees, sweat pants, all kinds of loose clothing, some with soft shoes and others without shoes, mill around the room talking quietly or practicing various exercises. The t'ai chi teacher comes into the room and says, quietly, "All right. Let's begin." The students take positions on the floor, and the class starts.

This is quite different from many of the Japanese martial-arts classes, where students line up according to rank and bow to the teacher. While there is a system of ranking in t'ai chi based on the student's skill and the length of time in training, colored belts are not issued (as in the Japanese system). Students know who the senior students are, and they are respected as such.

This class begins with a standing meditation exercise. The practitioners stand with their feet a shoulder width apart, parallel to teach other, and their knees bent in line with their toes. Their hands are held out in front of them as if they are holding a barrel, with their palms facing in. Their backs are kept straight. By holding this position and doing special breathing and mental exercises, the students work on awakening their ch'i. After perhaps five minutes of this special warm-up, they practice other variations of this exercise for five or ten minutes more before they begin their t'ai chi form. No stretching or strengthening exercises are done before the form, because all necessary exercise is contained within the form itself.

The T'ai Chi Forms

There are a few forms (or sets) in whatever t'ai chi style one might study, but all students usually begin by learning a first form which is done very slowly. Watching a person do the first t'ai chi form is like seeing someone move in slow motion. They move very, very slowly from one posture to the next in smooth, graceful motions. It may take as long as twenty or twenty-five minutes to complete one form. (Remember that a karate kata sometimes takes only thirty seconds to do.)

The primary purpose of doing the slow form today is to cultivate one's ch'i, tune up the body, and develop balance and coordination. It is also done as a kind of "moving meditation"—a mental exercise done in motion—which leads to peace of mind. Many of the ancient Chinese philosophers felt that meditation in motion was much better than meditation done just sitting in one spot. One old Taoist saying is: "The stillness

in stillness is not real stillness; only when there is stillness in movement does the universal rhythm manifest
itself." What this means in a very simple way is that it's
easy to be peaceful and calm if you're alone on top of
a mountain or deep in the woods, but try for that same
peace of mind while moving through the rush-hour
crowds in a city, or while sitting in the middle of your
screaming brothers and sisters. If you can feel calm
during this, then you have truly accomplished something. Moving through the form and striving for such
stillness is one aim of t'ai chi ch'uan.

The slow form can also be done for self-defense purposes, and every move can be used in fighting, although
many schools don't stress this aspect of t'ai chi today.
The graphic and poetic names given to various movements sometimes reflect the fighting aspects of the form:
"Snake Creeps in the Grass," "Carry Tiger to Mountain," and "Grasping the Bird's Tail." One does not, of
course, grasp any bird by its tail or carry off any heavy
tiger to a mountain, but instead, one makes a movement
that resembles what such an action might look like. The
animal gesture is just a symbol, and instead of learning
how to grasp a bird's tail, for example, the student is
really learning how to grasp the arm of an opponent in
a fighting situation. Sometimes the names of the moves
are clearer and leave little question as to their meaning:
"Turn Around and Kick with Right Sole," or "Strike
Ears with Fists."

The history of this slow-motion form is very interesting, for it was not always performed as it is today. Once
it was done as fast as the other kung fu sets. According

to legend, the form was changed by none other than Yang Lu-ch'an. It is said that the Manchu emperor, hearing that t'ai chi ch'uan had powers to bring longer life, summoned Yang to the palace to teach him the art. Yang, meanwhile, had secretly decided to teach the emperor a slightly different kind of form. He thought, "If I slow down the form somewhat, it will be easier to teach the emperor, who will certainly be angry with me if he doesn't learn it easily." Since the emperor was a Manchu—a foreigner who was ruling China—Yang decided that by changing the form somewhat he could keep from teaching the Manchu all the parts of t'ai chi, which Yang would then preserve for his own people.

This slow-motion Yang-style form eventually became very popular, and as the years went by more and more people began to study it. When more peaceful times came to China, and people trained more for health than for self-defense, the form was gradually simplified even more. The original Chen form that Yang once learned had many difficult jumps and leaps that required great acrobatic skill. In a typical move students would leap into the air, do a flying kick, and then land on their hands, doing another kick before they touched the ground. Many of these more difficult moves were taken out so all kinds of people, including those neither young nor strong, could also practice the form. In addition, the number of movements in the form was reduced. While the original Chen form had eighty-one moves, shortened forms today sometimes have as few as twenty-eight moves.

The key points of the form were retained over the

T'ai chi ch'uan movements: Carry Tiger to Mountain (top); Snake Creeps in the Grass (bottom).

134

years despite all the changes. While the slowness was originally only a teaching device, it turned out to be very valuable indeed. It would surely be misleading to think that the slow form is ineffective, or simple to do. The t'ai chi slow form is good for one's health because it puts to use every part of the body. There are some 710 muscles in the body, and this form, if done correctly, exercises all of them equally. Furthermore, all the movements of the form, the twisting, turning, and leg, arm, and waist movements, give a workout to internal parts of the body we would never think of exercising, such as the lungs, liver, stomach, and gall bladder. A slow movement is important because each time one does the movement, there is a great deal of action throughout the body. How could so much take place during a very fast movement?

Furthermore, it is not at all true that slow means easy. It might look easy, but try, for example, to get up from a chair in slow motion, or even harder, try sitting down in the same way. Do this without wobbling, with perfect control and balance, and you will see that slow can be very hard indeed.

This slow-motion form is a very popular exercise because it is graceful and interesting. No matter how much you work on it, you can always find more to perfect. Moreover, performing the form even one time every day is enough for maintaining good health. The form can be practiced alone, anywhere one wants—in the living room, by the river, or in an open field.

One does the form with a very relaxed body and a calm, concentrated mind that thinks about nothing else.

All t'ai chi movements are circular and are performed slowly, with one movement flowing right into the next.

All power comes from the waist area. The waist is like the center of a wheel, and the legs, hands, and elbows are like the rim of the wheel, moving only because the center moves. Concentration is kept in the tant'ien, that area two inches below the navel that is considered the warehouse of ch'i. The mind moves the ch'i from this spot, and the ch'i makes the hands, feet, and rest of the body move, as if it were a sort of fuel.

At the same time, one tries to breathe like a baby. While this may seem a strange idea, adults do, in fact, breathe differently from babies. A baby breathes naturally from the tant'ien, and if you watch, you will see its stomach area move in and out as it breathes. If you watch adults breathe, you will see it is their shoulders and chests that move. While all people breathe naturally from their abdomens when they sleep, adults have long since forgotten how to do this when they are awake. Those who want to do t'ai chi correctly must learn how to be in tune with nature once again.

While doing the form, the body must feel so very light that even the weight of a tiny feather touching it will be felt. The body must feel light in the air the same way it feels light in a swimming pool. T'ai chi can even be thought of as a sort of "dry" swimming, and after a while one can actually begin to feel the air just as one can feel water in a pool. At the same time, and this may seem like a contradiction, one's feet must feel rooted in the ground. If the form is done correctly, one should feel as if one's weight had penetrated below the surface of the earth.

These are just a few pointers to be kept in mind while doing the form. If one can do all these things at once, then on finishing the form, one will feel very good—not at all tired, but rather energetic and warm all over from one's fingers to one's toes.

Push-Hands

When students finish practicing their slow-motion form in class they usually work with partners on various exercises, the most common of which is "push-hands," called *tui shou* in Chinese. Push-hands is a two-person set that uses techniques found in the first form. The partners face one another with their wrists and forearms touching. They move their hands, arms, and bodies in a prearranged circular fashion, maintaining contact with each other at all times.

The two people now practice Lao-tze's ideas on yielding. When person A pushes, B yields, and when B pushes, A yields. Both try to yield at exactly the time they are pushed, and only as far. They don't want to give way sooner or any more than they have to. In this practice, students learn to feel when their opponents are weak or off balance. It also helps them locate weaknesses in their own bodies that they would have difficulty finding if they worked out only by themselves.

There are several patterns of push-hands that students learn—sometimes using only one hand, sometimes two, and sometimes working the arms while moving across the floor.

No special pattern is followed in advanced sets, and students practice "free-style" push-hands. This free-style practice is a very different kind of exercise. The object is to *break* contact with your partner. You try to escape from your opponent's hands while the opponent tries "stick to" or keep contact with your hands. At the same time, you want to make sure you stick to your opponent's hands, and your opponent tries to escape from you. You can imagine how tricky and complicated this can be.

If one does this practice correctly, then one's touch remains soft and light, but it cannot be gotten rid of. Some liken the t'ai chi player's arm to iron wrapped in cotton. Because of this softness, one ancient name for t'ai chi was "cotton fist."

Through push-hands practice, one develops keen sensitivity to one's opponents, learns how to "become one" with them and "feel" what they are going to do next even before they do it. This kind of sensitivity was developed to its highest level, perhaps, by Yang Luch'an's second son, Yang Pan-hou. Pan-hou was said to have developed marvelous "sticking energy" and could follow people like a shadow. When Yang was sixty years old he accepted a special kind of challenge from a boxer. The boxer asked Yang to put his hand on the boxer's back and try to keep this contact without holding on, no matter where the boxer moved. The boxer proceeded to run and jump all over the place, doing fast turns and leaps, and moving in quick circles, but no matter where he moved, Yang's hand was always lightly positioned on his back. Finally, the boxer jumped to the roof of a small house, and was happy to see that Yang was gone. He turned around, smiling to himself, and there was Yang, still behind him, smiling back.

Advanced T'ai Chi Training

At higher levels of training, depending upon the particular school and style, students learn t'ai chi forms with swords, spears, and staffs. They practice more complicated two-person sets, as well as a more advanced solo form which is characteristically done much faster than the first form, and usually requires more acrobatic skill.

AIKIDO

Aikido's Founder

Morihei Uyeshiba, the oldest son of a Japanese farmer, was born in 1883. When he was twelve years old his father, Yoruku, was often beaten up by village thugs. Then and there Uyeshiba decided to become strong so someday he could fight off his father's attackers.

Young Uyeshiba trained on his own. He took long runs through the countryside every day, and practiced lifting heavy weights around the farm. He became very strong, and when workers carried eighty pounds of rice or radishes, Uyeshiba would carry twice as much. This was helpful, but occasionally the young man was difficult to handle. During rice-cake contests held in the village, villagers placed a big blob of specially cooked rice in a huge stone bowl, and then used a large hammer to pound the rice to just the right consistency. Usually only very strong people could do this pounding well. Uyeshiba, intent on showing his strength, mashed the rice, of course, but he also broke the hammer. Not content with this one feat, Uyeshiba went to other villages, offering his services. Although his intentions were good, he proceeded to break their pounders as well. Eventually people saw him coming and tried to figure out how to keep him away from the rice pounder without offending him. Many offered him tea and cake, and tried to think of interesting things to talk about. Maybe he would forget, they hoped.

Uyeshiba, now a strong five-foot-1-inch, 180-pound "tank," as some called him, was also rapidly becoming a skilled martial artist. As a teenager he had begun to study many different styles of jujutsu and Japanese fencing. He practiced so hard that before long he was teaching these arts to others.

One school that especially influenced him was the Daito jujutsu school, headed by master swordsperson Sokaku Takeda. Uyeshiba was so interested in learning this jujutsu system—founded by the famous twelfth-century general and hero Minamoto Yoshitsune—that he invited Sokaku to live in his own home. Here Uyeshiba studied in the traditional way, cooking rice and brewing tea for his teacher, running his baths, and cutting wood for his fires. In return Sokaku taught Uyeshiba all his wonderful jujutsu techniques. In 1916, Uyeshiba finally obtained his teaching degree in Daito jujutsu, a style also called *aiki-jujutsu.*

It is said that Uyeshiba, with his marvelous strength and martial-arts skill, wandered throughout Japan, armed only with a *bokken* (a wooden sword). Everywhere he went he fought many challenges, and whenever he found someone of superior fighting skill he stayed on and trained with them until he had learned all he could. He eventually became one of the greatest martial artists in all Japan. Strangely, at just this time, Uyeshiba began to worry about the meaning of the martial arts.

What does it all mean? he thought. Yes, I have trained for years and years and today I can beat everybody, but someday, when I am older, someone will beat me. That is certain. What then is all this martial-arts training for, if someday I will be defeated? There must be some other answer. Is there no way that one can win forever, without losing?

He had to know the answer. He trained harder and harder. He knocked on the doors of famous temples in search of the answer. He studied religions and philosophies. He went up into the mountains for years, thinking and thinking in the hope of finding the answer. Sometimes he meditated under waterfalls, hoping the waters would open his spirit to the answers.

Finally, one day in 1926 while he was taking a walk in a garden, Uyeshiba got his answer. Standing under a persimmon tree, wiping sweat from his face, he had a fantastic experience. In his own words: "I felt that the universe suddenly quaked, and that a golden spirit sprang up from the ground, veiled my body, and changed my body into a golden one." Suddenly he felt he understood everything, that he was totally at one with the universe and was strangely "enlightened." He knew, then, the true meaning of the martial arts. It was very simple. In true martial arts there is no winning or losing, for one is not concerned with overcoming an opponent by force. True martial arts are "love." They are meant to "keep the peace of the world," and to "protect and cultivate all beings in Nature." Done this way, there is no defeat in the martial arts. While Uyeshiba's understanding is difficult to express in words, it was so clear and meaningful to him that he cried with happiness.

Uyeshiba said that from that time on he felt that the whole world was his house, and that the sun, the moon, and the stars were all his own things. Overflowing with this new understanding and wonderful feeling, he gradually developed his own special martial art, quite different from Daito aiki-jujutsu. His new art, called aikido, was concerned with self-perfection, loving one's opponent, and being in true harmony with nature and the universe. Developing and using one's ch'i became a most important new idea.

During the 1930's, Uyeshiba taught aikido in Tokyo. Jigaro Kano, the founder of judo, was so impressed with Uyeshiba that he sent several of his top students to study aikido with him. When Japan entered the Second World War in the 1940's, Uyeshiba moved to a mountain hut with a few of his students, and here he trained and farmed peacefully for twelve years. After Japan's defeat in the war, however, Uyeshiba came down from the mountains in order to teach the sad and dispirited youth of Japan.

Uyeshiba's combination of excellent skill and high level of spiritual development made his aikido unbeatable. Once in the 1920's, when he was teaching at the Japanese Naval Academy, several of the students, thinking he was a fraud because his aikido looked too easy and effortless, decided to ambush him. One evening they waited in the bushes near the school for Uyeshiba to pass by. The sensei smiled as he approached, sensing the ambush. Suddenly the students attacked, and each in turn was sent flying through the air. Uyeshiba proceeded jauntily down the path, still smiling. When the startled but unharmed students picked themselves out of the bushes, they could not remember having touched the master, or having been touched by him. How, they marveled, could Uyeshiba have thrown them?

As Uyeshiba got older he got even better. Some say that from the time he was fifty years old no one ever touched him. No matter how one attacked him, Uyeshiba was so good one could literally not lay a finger on him. Moreover, when Uyeshiba was in his eighties, and weighed a mere 125 pounds, he was still able to throw his students. As the story goes, he would come to his dojo to conduct class but, unable to climb the stairs because of his old age, would have several students lift him up to the dojo. Once on the dojo floor, however, he could send these same students flying all over the room.

Despite this extraordinary skill, Uyeshiba always felt

there was more to learn in aikido. He said, "Go as far in it as we will, there are no limits. Like the universe, aikido is without bounds. I am but a first-year student in aikido. I am studying now."

After Uyeshiba's death, several styles of aikido developed as offshoots of his original style. Today there are three main schools. Those of Gozo Shioda and Kenji Tomiki emphasize the more practical, self-defense aspects of aikido. Uyeshiba's main branch was inherited by his son Kisshomaru Uyeshiba and carries on the ideas of the father. It is more spiritual, less practical, and more popular with the general public.

The Principles of Aikido

We are all different. We are fat, short, skinny, wide, dark, tall, light, soft, and hard. This too is how we usually think of ourselves. We are aware of our physical bodies. Every day we wash our ears, put socks on our feet, medicine on our cuts, a hat on our head, and then look at the whole thing in the mirror. We may take our body outside to run, dance, or play because this makes our body feel good. Later we bring it home and give it a nice fat hamburger.

Yet what about our mind? Because our mind doesn't have any special shape, or color, that people can see, we often forget we have one. It operates automatically. We do little to fix it up and keep it in good shape like our body.

Aikido, the Japanese martial art, believes the mind, too, needs to be taken care of—exercised and made strong—every day. Aikido players also believe the mind should be made to work together with the body. While this may sound easy, think of all the times you sit in one place—doing your homework, perhaps—while your mind wanders outside with your friends, or inside to the refrigerator. Aikido teaches that a mind coordinated with a body can make that body do fantastic things never thought possible.

An example of how powerful the mind and body are when used together is "the unbendable arm." Try this experiment with a friend. First, make a fist and put strength into your arm, bending it up a little at the elbow. Then ask your friend to try to bend your arm the rest of the way. You can resist as hard as you want. Since your friend is allowed to use both hands, she or he will probably not have much trouble bending your arm.

Now, take the same position, only this time open your fist and don't put any strength at all into your arm. Relax your shoulder and elbow completely. Instead, pretend that your arm is like a fire hose, and that waves sent from your mind, like water, are flowing with terrific force through your arm. These powerful waves flow out of your hand and fingertips straight to the ends of the earth without stopping.

If you can really imagine this, really believe this is true, then your friend will find it very difficult to bend your arm. If you think "Oh, this will never work," or you lose concentration for even a second, then it won't work.

Another experiment of this kind can be done with

your whole body. Just stand in one place and have a friend or friends lift you up off the ground. Then, stand in the same place, close your eyes, and think of sending your mind power down through your body, through your feet, deep into the center of the earth. If you can keep up this concentration without breaking it, your friends won't be able to budge you from the spot.

Don't give up if you can't do these successfully the first time. Practice getting your mind and body working together a little bit every day, and then try again.

What is at work in these two experiments is ch'i. Everyone has ch'i, but it is only when we can get our minds and bodies working together that we can use and control our ch'i flow. When one thinks of sending one's mind waves or mind power out though the hand, one is in fact learning how to "pour forth ch'i."

Learning how to use ch'i is often a matter of *un*-learning many other things. Once we all had a natural flow of ch'i from the universe to us, and it flowed in turn from us to the universe. Just as a baby knows how to breathe naturally, so too it knows how to use its ch'i. As people grow up, however, they tighten up, develop new habits, and gradually forget how to keep this natural ch'i flow. As a result, babies can sometimes do things adults cannot. They can, for example, keep their tiny fists closed so that they are almost impossible to open. Adults, however, can do this only with great effort. It is usually only during a crisis, or when under hypnosis, that adults can tap this hidden power and do extraordinary feats they could not do otherwise. Luckily, there is another way for adults to regain this natural power. They can study aikido, which means "the way of bringing together one's ch'i." In aikido one practices a system of self-defense based primarily upon developing and controlling one's own and other people's ch'i.

Studying Aikido

Mats cover the floor of the aikido dojo where students congregate before class, wearing judo or karate type gis and sometimes *hakama*s, traditional Japanese wide-flowing pants which look like long skirts. They begin class, as in judo or karate, by lining up according to rank and bowing to their sensei.

As in t'ai ch'i ch'uan, aikido classes usually don't do rigorous warm-ups and strengthening exercises. Building muscular strength or overexerting in any way is not stressed. Instead, they do exercises for turning on and tuning up their ch'i.

If one wants to learn how to keep one's ch'i turned on while moving one's body, then it is important to practice an exercise which looks like mowing the lawn. In this exercise one moves back and forth with one's hands in front as if grasping a lawn mower. While moving, one practices special breathing, keeping one's concentration on the tant'ien area (called the "one point" in aikido), and sending one's ch'i from the hip area out through the wrists.

Other common warm-up exercises are designed to make the wrists stronger and more flexible, since many aikido techniques use the wrists for various holds and locks. Students—especially new ones—also practice rollouts that look something like somersaults. This is done so they won't hurt themselves when thrown by a partner. Other kinds of exercises done at the start of class are usually variations on these.

Aikido Techniques

Next the sensei shows the students the techniques she or he wants them to practice that day. Students then take partners and begin to practice, with one person acting as the attacker and the other the defender. Later, they switch roles. In a typical class students might work on three different techniques over and over again.

There is also aikido "free play." One defender stands in the middle of the floor and is attacked by the students in the class, one after another. The person must defend against each attack using various aikido techniques. Black belts sometimes practice this defense against two or three people who attack all at once. Sometimes the attackers even use weapons.

In contrast to some other martial arts, including t'ai chi ch'uan, there is no empty-handed kata practice in aikido. There are, however, sword-and-staff katas in the system.

It is somewhat difficult to explain in words what an aikido technique is like. It might help to explain first what it is not, and how it differs from the other martial arts we are familiar with. Unlike judo, for example, there is little grabbing or pulling on the opponent's gi, since throws are not done in this way. Moreover, there is no wrestling on the mat as there is in judo. In contrast to many karate styles (yet similar to t'ai chi ch'uan), movements in aikido are usually circular. Whereas much karate kicking and punching is done in a straight line, aikido techniques are often performed with the body moving like a spinning top. There is little emphasis on blocking, kicking, or punching.

Aikido's movements, based largely upon traditional Japanese fencing (*kenjutsu*), are quite different. To see more clearly just what aikido is, let's look at how a judoka, a karateka, and an aikido player would handle the same attack.

Let's pretend that all three persons are attacked by someone punching at them. Both the judoka and the karateka would probably stop the punch by blocking it. The judo player might then grab the attacker's arm, twist around, and throw the attacker with a crash to the mat. The karateka might follow the block by punching or kicking the attacker. But the aikido player, following Taoist principles, would try at all costs to avoid this type of conflict. She or he might use a technique called *yokomen-uchi ude-osae* (Oblique Strike Arm Pin). Instead of blocking the punch, the player would step to the side very quickly, getting out of the way of the punch altogether. Then, instead of hitting or throwing the attacker (although players sometimes do throw), the aikido player would connect with the attacker's elbow and wrist, not resisting but rather moving with the attacker's direction and strike momentum, and then would gain control and "lead" the attacker to the

Aikido technique: Oblique Strike Arm Pin.

ground. Now the player would apply an arm bar, keeping the attacker under control on the mat. This arm bar might be painful to the attacker, especially if he or she tries to get away, but after the aikido player let go, there would be no real harm done.

What is unique to aikido is this: When one does this exercise, or any technique for that matter, one is not only "leading" the opponent's arm or body, but one eventually learns how to actually "lead" the ch'i of the other person by "blending" with their ch'i, and becoming one with it. It is almost as if someone attacks not only with her or his physical self, but also with this invisible force—the same force that you practiced sending out through your "unbendable arm." If the defender can grab hold of this invisible force shield then they can really control their attacker.

When an aikido practitioner is very advanced, they can do this kind of "leading" with just one finger, and sometimes without even touching the body of their attacker at all.

Tournaments and Rank

In contrast to karate and judo, aikido has not developed into a popular competitive sport. Since a true aikido player does nothing unless attacked first, it would be hard to have a competition. Each player would sit waiting for the other to attack, and nothing at all would happen. While there are occasional competitions in some styles of aikido, students are judged according to how well they do a particular technique, as in karate or judo kata competition. There is a ranking system in aikido, similar to the judo system, with kyu and dan rankings. Some schools wear colored belts, while others do not.

Principles to Remember

While performing aikido the practitioners always try, just as in t'ai chi ch'uan, to keep in mind Lao-tze's ancient and very wise ideas about softness, yielding, avoidance, and nonaggression. At the same time, they always attempt to keep their concentration centered on the tant'ien. Next, they always remember those principles used in the unbendable-arm experiment. They try to relax completely, project their minds out through their arms, and in this way keep pouring forth their ch'i. They try to use no muscle, and to have no tension in their bodies. They must never be concerned with winning or losing, or be afraid of their opponent.

5 KENDO

According to legend, at the beginning of time the sun-goddess Amaterasu sent her grandson down to Japan. He carried with him three special things—a bronze mirror, a necklace of jewels, and an iron sword. Since that time, these items have had a special importance to the Japanese people. The sword, especially, has even been called "the soul of Japan."

Of all the weapons used by the samurai warriors in Japan's feudal age, the sword was the most loved and respected. Samurai would not go anywhere without their swords, and usually they wore two of them, a long one and a short one.

Like King Arthur's sword, this weapon was believed to have divine and magical powers of its own, carrying with it either good or bad fortune. A great sword was a family treasure, passed on from generation to generation like a fabulous jewel. Often it was considered a work of art, and the makers of swords great artists. They forged these magic, razor-sharp swords with age-old rituals and secret family techniques. The best of these exquisite weapons are preserved in museums, as admired as the works of Michelangelo or Leonardo da Vinci.

No less revered than the sword makers were those who sharpened and polished these beautiful weapons, keeping them in top condition. An expertly made sword needed an expert polisher. If swords were of poor qual-

Samurai, c. 1773. By Shunsho. Warrior Near Seashore.
                                  By Shunko, 18th century .

ity, top-notch polishers would refuse to fix them. If swords were of too great quality, the polishers would also refuse, knowing the swords were too great for them and beyond their abilities.

It is no wonder that very special customs surrounded the use of these precious swords. Samurai had strict rules about how to take a sword out of its scabbard and how to put it back. No other way would do. Stepping over someone's sword that was lying on the ground was a terrible insult, possibly resulting in the loss of one's head. Touching another's sword without permission was also an awful blunder. Only samurai had permission to wear swords at all.

The "art of the sword" that the samurai practiced was called *kenjutsu, ken* meaning "sword" and *jutsu* meaning "art." It was such a popular martial art that

The Swordsmith. *By Hokusai, 18th century.*

by the year 1600 there were thousands of different schools and styles of kenjutsu in Japan. Sword wielders practiced their art in kata form but tested their skills in real combat where people were often killed or maimed.

In addition, warriors were usually expert in using smaller blades, such as the dagger. Female samurai, especially, always carried a small dagger tucked away in their clothes, and often became the experts in *tantojutsu*, the art of the dagger. They were so adept at using this weapon that they could throw with accuracy even in the dead of night.

The samurai's fighting style and spirit were strongly influenced by the philosophy of Zen Buddhism, the Buddhism that was started in China by the famous Bodhidarma of Shaolin. One idea of this philosophy was called "mind of no mind." This meant that while in combat true swordspeople "emptied" their minds of all thoughts. They did not "think" about what cut to make with their sword, where to put their left foot, or how fierce the opponent looked.

This idea is not so strange if we think of ourselves riding a bicycle. After one learns how to ride a bike, it is far better *not* to think about how to peddle, how to steer, and how to keep one's balance. If one "thinks" about all these things at the same time, one is sure to fall off the bike. In the same way, samurai learned sword techniques in practice, and then in combat did their best to totally empty their minds. In this state of "no mind," they were able to develop and use their intuition, their "sixth sense." Without this heightened awareness, no samurai ever became a great sword fighter. They could

Small samurai running. By Kuniyoshi, 19th century.

always be caught off guard, for they were too busy thinking about something.

A famous story illustrates this Zen idea. Once there was a famous kenjutsu master who had three sons, all of whom trained diligently in the art of the sword. One day they were visited by an old family friend who was also a famous sword master. The father, eager to show off his sons to the old friend, decided to set up a test. The two masters went into the living room, where the father placed a jar full of water over the doorway. It was positioned so that it would fall on any person who opened the sliding doors and came into the room. While the two men settled down for tea, the father called his youngest son. Soon the boy came dashing through the door to find out what his father wanted. The jar started to fall, but the boy sensed danger, looked up, drew his sword, and cut the jar in half before it hit the ground. The father, turning to his friend, said, "This boy, standing here covered with water, is my youngest son. He is technically quite skilled with his sword, but as you can see, he still has a lot to learn."

After they had cleaned up the scattered pieces of pottery, the father placed another jar on top of the door and summoned his second son. Walking calmly through the door, the second son quickly stepped to the side, catching the falling jar without spilling a drop. He carefully replaced the jar, then turned to his father and asked him what he wanted. The father introduced the second son to his guest. "Oh yes, my second son has come far in his training, but he too has more to learn."

Then they called the oldest son. The two masters

drank their tea, waited and waited, but there was no response. Finally, the guest turned to the father. "Excellent," he said. "I commend you on teaching your son so well. Soon he'll be a fine sword master." Laughing, they both got up off their cushions, walked to the door, and took down the water jar. Sliding open the door, they saw the oldest son standing outside waiting with a big grin on his face. He had that sixth sense to know of the danger beyond the door. His skill went beyond his physical ability.

Using such Zen awareness and superb technical skill with their swords, countless samurai warriors went to battle, century after century, fighting for their various warlords. One famed swordsperson was the twelfth-century hero Yoshitsune Minamoto, the same person who originally founded the Daito school of aiki-jujutsu, the forerunner of aikido. People have created such miraculous stories about his youth that it is hard to know what is true, and what is not. Legend has it that Yoshitsune and his brother, orphaned at a young age, were taken in by warrior monks of Mount Kurama called *Yamabushi*. These monks, who were almost superhuman in their fighting abilities, and who often used magic in their techniques, carefully trained Yoshitsune in kenjutsu and the other martial arts. To make the training more difficult, these wizards kept using their magic against Yoshitsune. The boy might swing his sword at one of the monks, and in the next instant the monk would mysteriously vanish before the boy's eyes only to reappear suddenly in the treetops. Yoshitsune would then shoot an arrow at the laughing monk, who would easily brush it aside with his fan. Training against such elusive and clever characters, Yoshitsune eventually developed spectacular speed, technique, and awareness. In time, he became a formidable, almost superhuman swordsperson and a master of many other martial arts.

When Yoshitsune grew up, he became a kind of Japanese Robin Hood, drawing to himself a group of loyal and brave warriors who fought with his Minamoto forces. The most famous of his group was a huge monk named Benkei, who was somewhat similar to the Little John of the Robin Hood tale.

According to legend, Yoshitsune and Benkei met when Yoshitsune was just a young boy. Benkei, a warrior skilled in many fighting arts who always enjoyed a good fight, had decided that he wanted to collect no less than a thousand swords. Stalking the streets at night with his long curved spear (called a *naginata*), he preyed upon people out alone and bullied them out of their swords. Most were afraid to fight with the Hercules-sized character.

When Benkei had 999 swords in his collection, he set out for his final conquest. Early one morning he spotted a small veiled figure playing mournfully on a flute. The flutist began to cross a bridge and walk in Benkei's direction. Benkei noticed with surprise that the person carried a beautiful sword. Disappointed that this final conquest would be so easy, Benkei approached nonetheless. Seeing that his victim was just a young man of about twenty years, Benkei said smugly, "Okay, sonny, I want your sword. Just put it down on the ground here, in front of me, and be off with you." Much to Benkei's surprise, the lad paid no attention and just kept on walking, playing his flute as if he'd heard nothing. Angrily waving his naginata, Benkei said, "Okay, this is it. Hand it over or I'll have to hurt you." But the flute music continued to float over the still morning air. Now furious, Benkei swung his naginata, determined to strike the boy. Little did he know that the "lad" was none other than Yoshitsune.

Jumping up on the railing of the bridge, Yoshitsune avoided the strike completely. Benkei swung his long weapon again. Yoshitsune disappeared, reappearing on the opposite bridge railing. Benkei swung and swung, faster and faster, twirling and twisting, but he couldn't touch the elusive boy. Before long, he was totally exhausted. Suddenly, Yoshitsune pulled out a small fan and threw it with great speed and skill, hitting Benkei on the head. With that, Benkei gave up. Overwhelmed by the superb skill of the young man, this burly samurai laid down his naginata and swore to serve Yoshitsune for the rest of his life.

There were many great masters like Yoshitsune during the centuries of Japan's civil wars. While their skills were exceptional, and their bravery and loyalty unsurpassed, their lives were often filled with danger and bloodshed. When peace finally came to Japan in the seventeenth century, the government, hoping to cut down on the violence in the country, forbade people to use their swords for settling arguments. They encouraged them to use the bokken, or wooden sword, instead. Unfortunately, people still succeeded in killing each other with this weapon.

Ushiwaka and Benkei on Gojo Bridge. *Woodblock print by Kuniyoshi, 1840.*

Finally, in the late 1700's, a weapon called the *shinai* came into use. This weapon, a lightweight mock sword made out of bamboo, was much less dangerous than the bokken. In the 1800's, training and sportslike contests with the shinai became very popular. Sometimes there were even contests between men armed with the shinai and women armed with a different weapon, the naginata. Audiences loved contests such as these, and paid admission to come watch.

To further ensure that people could train seriously against one another without getting badly hurt, instructors encouraged their students to cover their bodies with special armor. Along with their gi tops and haka-mas (divided skirts) players wore a *men*, a head protector with a face grill that looked like a baseball catcher's mask. On their midsection, they placed a *do*, a protector that resembled the front of a potbellied stove, but was sometimes lacquered and beautifully decorated. They wore a *kote*, which looked like a hockey glove, to protect their wrists and hands, and they wore a *tare*, a lower body protector resembling a thick apron.

Along with these changes, some schools began to call their training *ken-do*, the "way" of the sword, rather than *kenjutsu*, reflecting the change in emphasis from learning the sword in order to kill one's enemy to learning the sword, or shinai, for one's own discipline and self-perfection. It is said that in kendo, one learns how to "settle the problems of life without drawing the sword."

Kendo is still practiced by at least eight million people around the world. It is very popular in Japan, where it is practiced for both spiritual development and sport. Girls and boys often study kendo in school, and in gym class they often play and compete with shinais instead of with baseballs or footballs.

In modern-day kendo, students use essentially the same kind of armor and shinais that people used two hundred years ago. After putting on their armor, students practice trying to score against each other by hitting certain targets on the opponent's body. In kenjutsu one could strike anywhere, but in kendo points are given only for strikes to the head (*men*), wrist area (*kote*), sides of the chest (*do*), and the throat area. In order to score, the strikes must be fast and strong. They must convince the instructor or judge that if this strike had been done with a real sword, the opponent would have been done in. One must also kiai (shout the name of the

Kendo fighting. Japanese woodcut, 19th century.

target to be hit, like "men"), step with the feet, and hit with the shinai, all at the exact same time. A famous kendo maxim is "The sword, the mind, and the body are one." Winners in competition are those who can score two out of three points in a match.

Ranking in kendo is similar to that of judo and aikido, divided into black belt dan rankings and six kyu levels under black belt. In contrast to many other Japanese arts, there are no colored belts or other signs of rank.

As in the other martial arts, kata is also performed in kendo although it is not emphasized. It is usually performed with a bokken, and is done primarily to preserve the older traditions of the art.

If you were to watch a kendo tournament, you might feel as though you were in feudal Japan, watching armored samurai in battle. The pace is fast and furious, with bodies crashing, shinais hitting with thunderous noises, and kendo fighters shouting their loud and piercing kiais. Kendo is very exciting to play and to watch.

6 NAGINATA

Almost two thousand years ago, some Chinese travelers brought a new weapon to Japan—a long pole with a sword set in the end. This weapon was called a *quando* in Chinese, and was named after the famous Chinese general Quan Ti.

Many hundreds of years later, in the tenth century, when the samurai warriors began fighting on horseback most of the time, this ancient weapon became very popular. It was now called a *naginata* (meaning "long sword"), and the entire weapon was usually from five to nine feet long. The curved blade attached at the end was one to two feet long.

The naginata was very good in battle. Because it was so long it could reach opponents on horseback before they got too close. It was longer than the popular sword and could outreach one in a fight. A good warrior could also trick an opponent and whip the naginata around fast, using the pole end as a weapon. This weapon was not too good for close-in fighting on a crowded battlefield, or in places where there were many trees, for one needed a lot of room to use it.

There was plenty of open space in Japan, however, and for hundreds of years the naginata was carried by most well-equipped samurai. The weapon was so well liked, in fact, that from the fourteenth to the sixteenth centuries there were as many as 425 different schools

Women fencing with naginata and bokken. Japanese woodcut, 19th century.

where one could study the art of naginata, or *naginata-jutsu.*

One early figure responsible for making the naginata so famous was none other than Benkei, the bodyguard and companion of the great twelfth-century swordsperson Yoshitsune. Benkei was so expert with the naginata, and had developed such a reputation on the battlefield, that a Japanese Kabuki play was even written about him. It is said that Benkei was often left standing alone on the battlefield because everyone was too afraid to fight with him. He was apparently none too happy about this, wanting his chance to try out his skill against a tough, "worthy" opponent.

The fame of the naginata was by no means limited to Benkei's exploits. It was for good reason that this weapon was sometimes called "the woman's spear."

During the third century A.D. women in Japan were very powerful. The first recorded histories of Japan tell of many warrior queens, like the priestess Himiko, whose name meant "Sun Princess." These women were so powerful that they ruled states and commanded their own armies against their enemies in Japan and across the waters in Korea.

From the tenth to the fourteenth centuries, when women had much of their earlier power taken from them, women of the samurai class still retained some authority. As part of their position, the samurai women were expected to be as excellent with weapons as the samurai men of their families. Starting when they were young girls, they were taught how to use several traditional weapons—the straight spear, the dagger, and, of course, the naginata. This long weapon was usually hung over the doors of every samurai household, and women were expected to protect their homes with it if necessary.

More than this, women were sometimes important warriors in their own right, commanding large numbers of men in huge battles. One such woman was Itagaki, a naginata master. She was a general in charge of three thousand warriors of the Taira clan, a group which refused to surrender to the more powerful Hojo clan. In the year 1199, when Itagaki and her forces were lodged at the family castle, they were suddenly attacked by ten thousand Hojo warriors who were determined to crush them once and for all. Itagaki courageously led her warriors outside the safe castle walls to take on the Hojo fighters. It is recorded that she rode on her warhorse expertly, guiding it skillfully with her knees, and at the same time wielding her razor-sharp naginata with amazing speed. Says one account: "She inspired her troops and shamed the enemy with her courage." Even though Itagaki's garrison finally lost to the superior numbers of the Hojo forces, the gallant Itagaki was long remembered and respected by both sides for her courage and great skill.

Another famous woman warrior of the same period was named Tomoe. The name means "circular" or "turning," and it was probably given to her because of her mastery of the naginata, which is used by making circular movements. It is said that because she was also strong and adept with the bow and arrow, and a marvelous horsewoman as well, many samurai avoided her in battle and picked other opponents to fight. On the battlefield she was absolutely fearless, and was said to be a match for one hundred warriors. Old Japanese writings, *Tales of Heiki*, say about her: "Many times she had taken to the field of battle armed at all points, and won matchless renown in encounters with the bravest captains. And so, in this final battle, when all others had been slain or fled, there rode Tomoe. . . ."

One hundred years ago, during the Satsuma Rebellion of 1877, one of the last civil wars in Japan, a battle was fought with a group of five hundred women in its ranks. These women, armed with naginatas, fought against the Japanese government troops. Unfortunately, their opponents were armed with guns, and although these warriors fought bravely with their naginatas, they were no match for these modern weapons and were defeated.

By this time people throughout much of Japan had already started to use the naginata for purposes other than warfare. As far back as the 1600's, with the dawn of a more peaceful period in Japan, more and more women began to study the naginata. Now, however, they did so to keep themselves strong and disciplined while there were no wars to fight. If no wild-eyed samurai were attacking their territory and they had no practical reason to work hard on their weaponry, then women as well as men were in danger of sitting around too much, talking, drinking tea, and getting lazy. Because of this, the study of practical naginata-jutsu gradually gave way to many schools of *naginata-do*—naginata practiced mainly for physical health and character building. This new form of martial art was studied mainly by women.

Fitting into this new scheme, a mock weapon was developed, just as one had been for kendo. Moreover, protective equipment, also similar to kendo armor but with the addition of *sune-ate*, or shin guards, was developed. It was also during this period that matches were set up on a regular basis between kendo practitioners and naginata practitioners. It even became fashionable for women to engage men in regulated contests.

In the late 1800's and early 1900's, naginata became so popular that it was even taught to young girls in the public schools.

Today in the high schools, colleges, and private

dojos of Japan, there are approximately two million women who practice naginata for both sport and spiritual development. The mock weapon that they fight with is usually an oak pole, six and one half feet long, with a twenty-one-inch bamboo blade at the end, covered by a leather cap at the tip. The players' protective armor is basically the same as that used hundreds of years ago.

There are currently several important schools of naginata in Japan, most of them descended from schools founded centuries ago. The one school with the greatest following is called Jikishinkage ryu, and was founded by Yamada H. Mitsumori. Other well-known schools are Tendo, Toda Buko ryu, Shinkage ryu, Katori ryu, and Ryushin Kan (Willow-heart school), headed by a husband and wife, Shohitsu Nakajima and Yumiko Nakajima. The woman, Yumiko, is the holder of an eighth-degree black belt in naginata.

As in any martial art, students practice their basic moves—in this case, thrusting, cutting, blocking, and parrying—over and over again, year after year. Naginata players try to hit their opponents with a good strong blow in certain special spots. Just as in kendo, they can hit to the opponent's head, wrists, and chest. In naginata, though, they can also attack to the shins.

To practice hitting their targets well, students sometimes work out against a life-size dummy in the dojo. This saves wear and tear on their opponents. Players compete in contests against opponents armed with naginatas, and sometimes with bokken. Practi-

Women in full modern armor practicing naginata.

tioners also study additional techniques through katas.

Naginata is a very exhilarating martial art. Despite the use of a bamboo blade instead of a metal one, the naginata is considered one of the most difficult martial-arts weapons to master. Today two million women carry on the Japanese women's fighting tradition through the practice of naginata.

7 NINJITSU

One of the most fascinating arts of all time was feudal Japan's *ninjitsu*. There is no exact translation of this word, but it is sometimes called "the art of sneaking in," "the art of stealth," or even "the art of invisibility." The people who practiced ninjitsu, called *ninja*, were in fact the first superagents, hired by the various warlords who were constantly feuding with each other. The ninja's jobs were to sneak into enemy territory, find out the secrets of the opposition, sometimes do destructive acts like setting fires or even assassinating enemies, and then escape without getting caught. In their trade these spies used weapons and tricks as ingenious as those employed by the James Bond character of today.

The art of ninjitsu has its very earliest beginnings in a Chinese classic, *The Art of War*, written two thousand years ago by a legendary Chinese general, Sun-tze. In the sixth century A.D., some of the tactics of spying outlined by Sun-tze and other military thinkers were finally introduced into Japan from China. Here they were studied and perfected by groups such as the Yamabushi, the same mountain-warrior priests who taught the famous Yoshitsune. Eventually, beginning in the twelfth century, ninjitsu began to emerge as a highly developed art, and for the next four hundred years it flourished as an independent art in its own right.

Not just anyone, however, could become a ninja, for ninjitsu was a secret art, practiced only by certain families. It was passed on in the greatest secrecy from one generation to the next, and few from the outside were allowed to learn it. Most ninja families lived in remote mountainous areas of Japan, and their simple-looking farmhouses were filled with secret passageways, sliding panels, and trapdoors.

Girls and boys of ninja families began training as spies when they were just five or six years old. From the very start they were taught to become great athletes— to swim, dive, jump very high, run fast and long, ride horses, and climb everything from trees to castle walls. Training was very, very hard in order to prepare these young ninja for the difficult work of later years. It is said they would hang by their hands from tree branches for a long time in order to develop both strong arms and strong minds. They practiced holding their breath, and also staying in one spot without moving for a long time. When they were twelve or thirteen years old they began learning weapons and practiced running. It is said that an adult ninja could run over a hundred miles without resting.

In the tradition of the great spies, the ninja paid much attention to keeping their identities secret. We don't know the names of most of the famous ninja just because they never told anyone who they were. They used many different names in a lifetime, and some had many separate identities. The same man might be a carpenter in one town, an artist in another, and a blind man in a third. One woman might have three different families in three separate provinces just to keep everyone confused. The ninja was especially feared because no one ever knew when he or she might meet one. It could be the farmer down the street, the singing courtesan, the fish seller, or one's best friend.

Making matters more complicated, ninja were also masters of disguise, and could quickly change their appearance when it was necessary. Men often dressed up as women, and women as men. It is no wonder that the historical records don't help us much in trying to figure out who was who in the ninja ranks.

Ninja were also highly skilled in the arts of illusion. It was believed they could transform their bodies into animal forms, or become invisible at will. Such stories were terrifying, but in fact such feats were just tricks of the trade. When ninja were being hunted down in the woods, for example, they might have with them, hidden in their capes, a monkey dressed exactly like themselves. At just the right moment they would turn the monkey loose, then quickly climb a tree. The pursuers, seeing this monkey dressed like the ninja, would give up the chase and run, terrified, out of the woods, sure that the ninja had turned into a monkey.

Ninja could become "invisible" using the special clothes they wore. They wore different-colored clothing that blended with their surroundings, giving the illusion they had disappeared. They wore all black at night, and all white in the snow, for example. Sometimes they would jump into a river or pond, where they would stay underwater for a long time, breathing out of a bamboo tube. They might roll up into a ball, giving the appearance of a stone, and remain there for hours, motionless on the landscape. They could cling lizardlike to a wall, or position themselves so they looked like the limb of a tree. Stuck in an open field, they might stick out their arms and pretend to be scarecrows.

We can certainly understand why people called ninjitsu "the art of invisibility." While these tricks may seem old hat to us today, we should remember that hundreds of years ago they were new and very clever tricks that easily fooled people.

Like the great Houdini, the ninja women and men were also great escape artists. From earliest childhood they learned how to dislocate the joints in their body so they could actually slip out of ropes and knots if they were captured and tied up. In the secret pockets of their clothes, or hidden in their hair or ears, they carried little tools that could be used to pick locks.

Ninja were called "human flies" because they could climb anything, including castle walls, by using all kinds of ladders, hooks, and foot and hand attachments. They "flew" by using their capes as parachutes, and sometimes even attached themselves to huge kites in order to "hang glide" over walls into enemy territory. Ninja could also "walk across water" by using special rafts, shoes, and types of life jackets.

In addition to all these skills, the ninja were experts in all the traditional martial arts of the time, such as jujutsu, kenjutsu, naginata-jutsu, the staff, and the bow and arrow. However, they used these traditional weapons and arts in all kinds of strange and unexpected ways. They would set fire to arrow tips and shoot them into enemy camps. The staff they carried sometimes had a hollow end concealing a knife, a chain, or some chemicals that could be blown into an enemy's face.

Ninja also had their own special arsenal of weapons. When they were pursued they would pull out of their pockets special pointed weapons that looked like stars or "jacks." When they threw them on the ground, they always landed with one sharp point facing upward. The unsuspecting pursuers would step on these *tetsu-bishi*, as they were called, and give up the chase. The ninja also stuffed their pockets with *shuriken*, sharp-pointed weapons shaped like stars or crosses that could be thrown like darts at people. They would also hold tiny dirks in their mouths and blow them at the enemy, or shoot poison darts through blowguns. To distract opponents, they would use smoke bombs and firecrackers— terribly frightening to people who had never seen or heard of gunpowder. Women, or men disguised as women, used all the above weapons, plus very long and sharp hairpins to prick their unsuspecting enemies.

Not only did the ninja know how to use all these weapons with perfect accuracy, but they were also their own pharmacists. They made all their own poisons to go on the tips of their weapons or into others' tasty meals. Some poisons would kill their enemies, while others would put them to sleep, make them itch, or just make them laugh. Ninja mixed all their own explosives, and even made their own medicines. A secret agent couldn't afford to risk her or his identity by visiting a doctor.

Well-equipped ninja on a mission carried everything with them. They were surely good magicians, for they managed to look as though they were just everyday

Ninja with weapons (clockwise from top left): rope and bamboo climbing device; shuriken and pouch; tetsu-bishi (cal-trops); sword; rope with grappling hook.

farmers or shopkeepers. How they managed to conceal all their little weapons, food, medicine, ladders and hooks, a monkey, breathing tubes, rafts, explosives, poisons, smoke bombs, and various changes of clothing and facial disguises, to name just a few, is perhaps most miraculous of all.

Indeed, these ancient practitioners of ninjitsu were marvelous, and there seems little question that they were the greatest superagents of all times.

ACKNOWLEDGMENTS

Page 14: The New York Public Library Picture Collection.

Page 43: *Tomoe Gozen Killing Uchido Saburo Ieyoshi*, by Toyonobu (1711–1785). Book illustration, c. 1750.
The Metropolitan Museum of Art, Samuel Isham Gift, 1914.

Page 45: From an illustration by Masanobu Tsukioka (Settei) (1710–1786) in *Women of Military Prowess*, 1766.
Toyo Gallery, Inc.

Page 45: Illustration by Masahiro Murai from A *Single Horseman: Summary of How to Wear Armor*, Yedo, 1735.
The Metropolitan Museum of Art.

Page 47: Illustrated book of sword combat, 1764. From *Arms and Military Art Japan 1546–1906*.
The Metropolitan Museum of Art.

Page 122: The Bettman Archive.

Page 154: *Second Ichikawa Yaozo as a Sumurai*, by Shunsho, c. 1773.
The Metropolitan Museum of Art, Pulitzer Fund, 1918.

Page 154: *Warrior near Seashore*, by Shunko (worked 1771–1791).
Metropolitan Museum of Art, Rogers Fund, 1922.

Page 155: *The Swordsmith*, by Hokusai (1760–1849). From *36 Poems by Artisans*.
The Metropolitan Museum of Art, Rogers Fund, 1936.

Page 157: Small samurai running, by Kuniyoshi (1798–1861). From album of 15 triptychs of famous battles.
The Metropolitan Museum of Art, Gift of Harold de Raasloff, 1918.

Page 162: *Ushikawa and Benkei on Gojo Bridge*, woodblock print by Kuniyoshi (1798–1861), 1840.
Museum of Fine Arts, Springfield, Mass. The Raymond A. Bidwell Collection.

Page 164: Kendo fighting. Middle panel of woodcut triptych on paper. 19th-century Japanese.
The Metropolitan Museum of Art.

Page 167: Women fencing with naginata and bokken. 19th-century Japanese woodcut.
The Metropolitan Museum of Art.

181

Format by Kohar Alexanian

Set in 12 pt. Times Roman

Composed and bound by The Haddon Craftsmen,
Scranton, Penna.

Printed by Rae Publishing Co., Inc.

HARPER & ROW, PUBLISHERS, INC.